I WON THE RACE IN MY MOTHER'S SHOES

I
WON
THE RACE IN MY
MOTHER'S
SHOES

DAMEAN ADAMS

Charleston, SC
www.PalmettoPublishing.com

I Won The Race In My Mother's Shoes
Copyright © 2021 by Damean Adams

First Edition

Hardcover ISBN: 978-1-63837-320-9
Paperback ISBN: 978-1-63837-322-3
eBook ISBN: 978-1-63837-321-6

Contents

Foreword

By Dr. Joseph O. Okpaku, Sr.

Everyone has a dream, and the extent to which each one succeeds in fulfilling that dream depends on many factors, most essential of which are our faith, the quality and extent to which we feel loved, our hope, tenacity and resilience, our innate talents and attributes, opportunity, our environment and context and our experience of childhood. Central to all of this are our parents and the extent to which they guide and nurture us and prepare us, emotionally, psychologically and mentally, to make the best of what life offers while coping and managing diligently and with confidence and equanimity, the challenges it presents to us. In this scheme of things, mothers are particularly significant because they are our first friend and companion at birth. Besides carrying us around, feeding us and subsuming all their interests to our wellbeing for the nine or so months before we are ready to emerge into the world, they nurture and protect us with their lives at a stage when we are essentially helpless, and groom us for the journey of life, uncertain about what lies ahead for us. For them, no sacrifice is too big to make for our sake.

And so, *I Won The Race In My Mother's Shoes* is a natural and worthy tribute to mothers everywhere, and to aunts, sisters, cousins, family and friends who in their various ways contribute each in her own way to our childhood, youth and older life. It is, indeed, also a tribute to fathers, uncles, brothers, male family and friends who made the enormous task of raising us a little easier and more wholesome by their assistance, care, love and affection. They too created a little space in their shoes so that we too can walk or run in them as we craft the trajectory of our own lives. The stories, actually the testaments that the contributions to this collection have shared, narratives of once clear dreams running into fog and the struggle to fight relentlessly until they could break through to the bright sunshine again, are moving, enlightening and sobering Yet in all cases they are reassuring tales of the victory of hope against the storm of despondence and the threat of defeat.

This book offers stories of the supremacy of faith and hope when we find ourselves swimming against the tide, not knowing what awaits us upstream. In each of their stories, the contributors pay tribute to their mothers and others who were there for them when they most needed someone to believe in them, have faith in them, and be willing to stake their own in support of them. Saying "thank you" to those who were there for us in such difficult times, is such an important thing to do, even when those who have made the sacrifices tell us there is no need to do so. We all need acknowledgement and positive reinforcement, not only in recouping from the sacrifices made, but in reinforcing out ability to fight even harder for the next person who needs us.

Against the tableau of joy, laughter, enthusiasm and celebration, life can be and is sometimes quite challenging, as is graphically captured by every single story in this collection. Each one tells the story of personal pain, anguish, trauma and the fear of failure, and how he or she survived or is surviving. In sharing their innermost experience, they show the kind of courage that people demonstrate when they wish that others learn from their experience or find courage in the knowledge that they are not alone. Every one of them deserves acknowledgement and gratitude for the courage to do so. Their stories and the lessons they hold constitute the quintessential value of this book, and that value is vast. It makes *How I Won The Race In My Mother's Shoes* a book everyone should read and share with those they love and care about. It is a book of courage that provides hope and inspiration.

Often, especially if we are of a positive disposition or see ourselves as being of a strong breed, we tend to camouflage our times of distress, partly because of our pride and sense of self-esteem, but often also because we genuinely do not wish to impose our private trauma on others. But most often, there are one or two people around us who know instinctively when we are down and out, our own attempts to disguise notwithstanding, and they are more than glad to help. The one group of people who are experts at this are our parents, especially our mothers, because in the months when they carried us in their wombs, they came to know us rather well as a matter of instinct. They do not need to see our faces or hear our voices for them to know that all is not well. That is the special attribute of parenting, especially of motherhood. For that, the contributors to this collection offer eloquent tributes in telling their stories.

In the title piece, the author/editor of this collection, Damean Adams, shares the story of early childhood in his native Jamaica, why and how the family migrated to the United States and the difficulties growing up in Mt. Vernon, New York. It is a story of the challenges of life and youth and the sacrifices of his mother and grandmother to keep the family afloat and him on a straight path. Damean's, is a familiar story of the experience of immigrant families in America. What makes the story even so touching, enlightening and memorable is its total candor. I had the opportunity of sharing and observing much of Damean's young years in Mt. Vernon at close range, as a close friend of the family. Damean was particularly close to me, and I had the privilege of serving as his close confidant. I watched the growth of his tenacity, focus, and quiet determination, and his limitless love and affection for his mother, his grandmother, his sisters and his aunts, together constituting the women who raised and groomed him, and his uncle.

We learn a lot from people around us. Some of it we realize at the time, some of it we recognize a long time afterwards. I watched Damean grow into a noble career in the U.S. Marines, becoming an officer and gentleman as the saying goes. I was very proud of him when he served abroad in support of the United States. Damean's embracing of faith and commitment to share its wholesome benefits with others, as most articulately demonstrated in his comments after each story in this book, especially given his very gentle nature, is a blessing to those who come into contact with him and share their hopes and dreams with him. Damean's own life story is an inspiration for those who happen to be with and around him. This is clear to me in reading all the stories in this book, especially his commentary at the end of each contribution.

I Won the Race in My Mother's Shoes

We didn't have the money—I was twelve years old using Elmer glue to hold the bottom of my shoe together. My Mother couldn't afford to buy me another pair until the beginning of the next school year, but I wanted to win this race!

It was my sixth-grade year in elementary school. Close to the end of the year, they would have a citywide mini-Olympics between all of the schools and have the students compete against each other. At the time, I knew I wasn't the smartest kid in my school, the only thing I did know at that time—I was the fastest. I called it a God-given talent, and good genes from my parents, even though I never really saw them run. Being Jamaican had a little role to play in it also I guess, since we are known for having some of the best and fastest track and field runners in the world.

I wanted to run the two-hundred-meter dash to represent my school, and hopefully bring the first gold medal in my school's history. The day before, all of the students who were going to compete we had to go see our gym teacher. He was a tall, serious man, who almost everyone was afraid of because he wouldn't say much, but when he did, it was as if he was a drill Sergeant in the army giving orders, and if you didn't obey, you were going to have to pay the consequences. We all got together, anxious to hear what race we would be running.

The year before, Mr. Hall, our gym teacher, put me on the 4x100 meter relay team. He'd said, "You can help the team win since you are the fastest." I had believed him, and I'd been determined to do it. The only problem, however, was, on a relay team, you had to rely on your teammates in order to win. We came in third, no matter how big of a lead I gave them from the first leg, at the end, we didn't win.

This was my last year to do this, so I figured he would have no other choice to put in the individual race other than me. He started to give out the assignments, and when he got to the two-hundred-meter dash, he called Tyrone, not Damean. My heart felt like a balloon that just burst in my chest. *I know I'm faster than Tyrone*, I furiously thought in my mind. Mr. Hall then called out the relay team members, and, of course, I was on it. He assigned me to be the anchor leg this year, he explained the importance of the leg, and how we could win. I was mad and wanted to tell him that he was making a big mistake. It seemed like déjà vu, I'd seen this movie already, and I already knew the outcome. I should've been the one running the two-hundred-meter dash, but I wasn't. I just accepted the fact and reality at the time, we may lose again.

It wasn't until a couple months later that I found out Mr. Hall was actually Coach Hall, the head coach of the high school girl's track team. I went home that day defeated, like I had already lost the race, the only person I wanted to talk about it with was my Granny. She was the one who could see any dark situation and put light on it. I remember telling her about the mini- Olympics and how I should have been running the 200, and it wasn't fair.

She looked me in the eyes and adjusted her eyeglasses. "Damean, life isn't always fair, the only thing that you can do is your best." Just like my Granny's cooking, when you eat it, you feel satisfied, and loved at the same time. I understood exactly what she was telling me.

I had one pair of shoes for the whole year to go to school, and I knew I wasn't going to have another until the next year. Using glue and putting a paint can on it to hold it down overnight was the only way it could dry in time for me to have it in the morning. When I was going for the paint can to put on my shoes, I saw my Mother's old pair of shoes she used to wear to work. They had a couple small holes in them from wear and tear, the sole was worn, but it was still on the shoe. My Mother worked long hours on her feet at the Woolworth store six days a week to provide for my sisters and I. She needed comfortable shoes to wear so that she could handle the long hours on her feet. The shoes where light brown with maroon stripes on them, but the best part of all, they were the closest thing to running shoes at that time. My mind started to race like a hamster on its wheel, and then the light turned on. I can wear my mother's shoes! I tried them on, and even though they were a little tight, they fit!

I waited up for my Mother to come home from work, and before she even had a chance to sit down from her long day, I was right there waiting with the shoes in my hand. I said, "Hi, Mom, can I borrow your shoes?" Without hesitation, she asked me why. I explained the story and the situation with my school shoes, and what I was doing to repair them. She went silent for a minute, it seemed as if she was disappointed, not in me, but in herself, for me only having one pair of shoes to go to school.

I waited for an answer, and even though she wasn't using them anymore, I still had a little thought in my mind that she may tell me no. I was surprised and happy when she told me yes. "If they fit you, and you feel like they will make you run faster, go for it." It probably wasn't the best motivational speech at the time, but because my Mother wasn't the affectionate type of person at that time, it was more than enough to get me motivated!

The morning of the race, before my mother left the house to go to work, she told me, "Good luck, and God be with you." My Mother always explained that it was God who gave you the wins or losses in life. I understand it so much better now as an adult than as a child. I knew I couldn't wear my mother's shoes to school because I would have to fight that day. I would've been the laughingstock of the school if I walked in with women's shoes on my feet. So, I put them in a plastic bag, put them in my backpack, and went to school.

Mr. Hall gathered us up all together so that we could get on a school bus to go to the stadium. I was looking excited, and nervous at the same time, but ready to run. Mr. Hall started to call out everyone's name to make sure we were all there. "Tyrone, Tyrone, has anyone seen Tyrone?" he asked. My ears came to full alert, and my eyes started to scan for Tyrone. One of the administrative ladies from the main office came out and spoke to Mr. Hall. It was loud enough that we all heard what she told him.

"Tyrone's Mother just called. He has the chickenpox!" To this day, I know I've never been so excited to hear that someone was sick! I said in my head, *Thank you, Jesus*, and then asked for forgiveness. I was thinking, *God, please let him put me in the two-hundred-meter dash*. I knew it wasn't right to desire to be an individual or selfish, but at that moment, the only thing on my mind was the gold medal.

Mr. Hall seemed a little annoyed with the news and said, "Thank you," and then looked at the clipboard he had in his hand. He made a couple marks with his pen and then made eye contact with me. He called me over to him and said the only words I wanted to hear that day, "I'm taking you off of the relay, and you are going to run the 200."

I responded with a confident, "Yes, sir," but in my mind, I wanted to hug him with excitement or at least give him a high five.

I took my mother's shoes from out of the plastic bag, looking around and hoping no one saw me. It was my time to run the trials of the two-hundred-meter dash. All of the runners for that heat were told to walk up to the starting line and make sure that our foot wasn't touching the line. I was nervous but excited, I looked at all of the boys ready to race, sizing up my competition. They all looked scared, so I knew then, as long as I didn't fall, I had a high possibility to win. The gun fired for us to go, and without trying, I started to move away from everyone. I won the trials, and a sigh of relief came over me. I got confident in the semifinals because of the experience of winning the trials. I knew at that moment that running was my gift, and I was meant to be there.

After winning the trials and semifinals, the kids from other schools started to talk. Eventually, the chatter reached me about the fastest kid from another school who won the gold medal last year. Everyone was saying that he was going to win, and no one is faster than him!

The confidence that I thought I had, and the sense of destiny, began to disappear. I got scared, a knot formed in my stomach, and then I thought I needed to use the bathroom. My nerves started to get the best of me. Would I lose, after all that had happened?

They called the runners to report to the starting line for the finals of the two-hundred-meter dash. One of the other kids said "good luck." I responded with an almost whisper and head nod, "Thanks."

We got our instructions from Mr. Hall, who was going to fire the gun for us to run. I knelt down on the grass before going on the dirt track to tighten my shoes. I pulled the lace of my Mothers shoes, choking my feet like a snake squeezing its prey. Even with all the fear, nerves, and the feeling like I needed to use the bathroom was still there, I wanted to win. I glanced over at the kid that they were all talking about, and he looked ready. He and I were about the same height, and the look in his eyes told me he was ready to fight. Everyone else at the time didn't matter to me, because deep down, I knew the race was only between the two of us.

"On your mark," we walked up to the line. "Get set," from my head to my toes, I was scared of the outcome. *Bang!* The gun went off. Because of the dirt track and minimum traction on my Mother's shoes, my first step slipped before I got traction, like a drag racer spinning its wheels. Once I got in motion, all of the fear, nervousness, the feeling of using the bathroom disappeared. I wanted to win, I wanted the gold, I wanted my Mother and my Grandmother to be proud.

I started running harder than I ever had before. My mouth was huffing and puffing like a blow fish trying to generate more air. I started pumping my arms like a runaway train, my legs started rising to my chest like a Thoroughbred champion horse. I was in what some runners call the zone—total focus. After crossing the finish line, there was so much dust and yelling from the stands of the schools cheering for their runner, I didn't even know who won the race. All I knew was I crossed the finish line by myself.

I won. I won! Nothing had a better feeling in life than the sense of accomplishment. Being at the top of the award stand was one of the best feelings in my entire life, to this day. I was so excited to let my Mother and Grandmother know that I had won! Later on, I found out I broke the record for that specific race.

I told this same story to a good friend of mine. He and I met when we went to one of our military training schools as a

Marine. We were reminiscing about our past, and some of the defining moments in our life. When I first started to tell the story, he didn't really know where I was going until the end of it. Silence went over the phone for a minute, then he said, "D, that is the title of your next book!" I was puzzled, not knowing what he was talking about, then he said, "I WON THE RACE IN MY MOTHER'S SHOES."

Instantly, I knew exactly what I had to do. Literally—I did win my race in my mother's shoes, but metaphorically, in my life, and all of the accomplishments from that point on, was to make my mother and grandmother proud. I've won multiple races in their shoes, because they raised me, gave me confidence, cheered me on, and loved me. Because of God and both of them, I did win the race in my mother's shoes.

However, when you think about it in a bigger picture, isn't this the story of millions of other people? Men and women alike who were raised by their mother, grandmother, aunt, or strong woman in their lives? These women didn't know how they were going to do it, but they never gave up and made it happen, learning how to be mother and father at the same time without instructions. This wasn't just my story, it's our story, and we have to tell it, and they need to hear it, before it's too late.

Acknowledgments

I would like to take this moment to say thank you! First, and always, thank you God, our Lord and savior, Jesus Christ! All that we are, all that we will ever be and become that is good is because of You. Our gifts, talents, and abilities that we have is because of You, and we strive each day to use them for good to serve You and Your people, Amen!

Thank you to all of the contributing writers who made this book possible. Also, thank you to all of the other writers who submitted their contributing stories. Even though they aren't in this version of the book, we're truly grateful and humbled to have you share your story with us.

Navida	Sean, O
Kimberly	Chris
Molly	Darryln
Sean, F	Edward
Amber	Johnny
K. P	Brian
Angela	Ambra

Hannah	Nadia
Danielle	Deb
Kat.W	Pat
Kobe	April

Your courage to share such private, intimate, and sacred parts of your life is something I could never thank you enough for. The life experiences that all of you have had and shared, we pray will give others courage, hope, and faith in themselves, in life, and in God—to know that they aren't alone, that they don't have to be silent any longer, that no matter what happened in the past, it doesn't have to define who they are.

Each of you have opened up a new opportunity for so many people to be grateful for the lives that they already have and the people they have and had in it. Thank you so much from the bottom of my heart! May God continue to love, guide, and protect you all with great health and success! God bless you!

I would also like to thank everyone who inspired us on this journey. To Gabriel and Elijah, to all of my family and friends who are near and far, we hope we are making you proud. My accomplishments are not mine, they're ours! I would not be here without all of your care, influences, prayers, and pushing us forward!

A special thank you to my mentors Tony, and Ken, thank you for all of your guidance, lessons, and truth in life, that has elevated my mind to think, and be different. You both are truly gifts from God, to help form my life, and many others.

An honorable mention goes to some of the most influential people that made an impact on our journey in life. Some didn't know they were doing it, but from the bottom of my heart, I'm blessed because of you. Thank you and God bless.

Donny Dendy	James Mattis
James Conway	Keith Stalder
Rodney Hardy	Derrick Fennel

To Dr. Joe Okpaku thank you for writing a magnificent forward, my editor Marni Macrae, and Erica Buday. You've all played such a big role in putting all of these stories together. Thank you so much, for helping us reach deadlines, keeping us focused, and cheering us on. And Thank you to Palmetto Publishing Group and their wonderful staff for helping us share this book with the rest of the world! May God bless you all!

Very Respectfully,

Damean

Introduction

Thank you for taking the opportunity to read this book, it has been an honor and a privilege to share this experience with some amazing people. This book was written because we all have a story in life.

For the majority of us, at some point in our lives, we've crossed paths with someone who said or did something for us. Someone who opened up our eyes, heart, or mind to a truth or led us down a different path than the one we were on.

Often, we didn't even know that what that person said or did would make such an impact until we were much older. In this book, each story is different. However, they all share one amazing thing in common—gratitude.

Our prayer is that there will be one or more stories that anyone can relate a part of their lives to, good or bad. These stories may make you cry, think, laugh, and we hope, in the end, be grateful for someone or everyone in your life.

All these stories are of real people who've had real experiences that changed their lives forever. It took a tremendous amount of bravery, courage, and love to share their chapter.

The stories contain times of hate, envy, physical and mental abuse, rape, torture, mental illness, and divorce, just to name a few. These stories were written not for judgment, but from the heart, from the soul, from truth. They aren't for accolades, but as a sign and symbol of freedom.

We hope it will give you courage and a sense of urgency to find the people who mean the most to you, and say thank you, I forgive you, and most importantly—I love you!

Our lives as we know it, clearer now more than ever before, isn't guaranteed tomorrow. The only thing that we have right now is this moment.

When we're born, the clock starts to our race in life. Everyone is running a race, whether we want to admit it or not. It doesn't matter who or what you are, time doesn't stop for anyone. It's the most valuable commodity that we neglect until we realize that we don't have enough of it.

Even though we're running a race, or multiple races, in life, each one of them are different. What separates us is our finish line. All of us have our own finish line! Our death marks the end of our race on earth.

Some of us are running a sprint, some mid-distance, and some a marathon. However, no matter how long or short our race is, there is always a finish line.

We never truly know when or where our finish line is, but we do know for sure that we will have one.

Because of this, we should strive to always remember to stay in our lane and run our race and not someone else's.

We must know that the race someone else is running is meant for them and them alone. We must never be jealous, envious, or try to get in the way of others. When we do, that is a sure way for us to disqualify or delay ourselves from winning the only race that we could win, the only race that we were born to win—our own!

So, the question remains; how do we know if we are winning our race! The only way for us to truly know this answer is by our efforts!

Because you're reading this right now, it's evident that we've all been given unique gifts, talents, and life to live!

How do we use these gifts and talents? And especially how do we give back, serve people, use them for good, and give God the credit!

We know that the race is not going to be easy, but we can't give up. We know that there will be times of frustration, hurt, anger, and the wanting to quit, but we must continue. We know it's hard when we look at others winning and we don't see hope for ourselves. We also know that because we were born, we were meant to win. If we look up to God, we'll find the strength within to endure the pain, to fight back when all is against us, to have faith that God is with us, and because of that—our race is already won!

CHAPTER 1

A Son's Love

My sisters and I were sleeping in our home in Jamaica. We heard screaming and an argument going on with our parents. My father came home drunk again, and my mother didn't like it.

Not knowing how it started or who started it, my father started to beat my mother. Shivering in fear of the unknown were my two sisters and myself. I was five years old at the time, and the youngest, as well as the only boy in my family. The screaming and fighting moved outside as my mother tried to get away from my father. He wanted a tool to take his bed apart so that he could leave, and my mother didn't know where to find it to give it to him. I'm sure he thought she was lying, which was why he kept on beating her.

My sisters and I crept slowly toward the noise, afraid, but needed to see what was going on. The beating continued, and my heart started to beat faster and faster out of fear. My mother was being beaten by my father before my eyes, and even though it may have happened before, this time it was worse because I was watching it happen. The tears of fear were coming down our eyes as my sisters and I watched the pain and hurt that our mother was in. I watched my mother try to get away from him, but he caught her again. My sisters and I couldn't take it anymore and had to show ourselves from hiding, hoping that he would stop. He didn't, no matter how hard or loud we cried and screamed.

In Jamaica, we lived in the country, and even though our neighbors might have heard the screams, they didn't want to get involved. What was perhaps a couple of minutes at that moment truly felt like hours of watching the person who birthed me being beaten without mercy. It continued, and even though my mother tried to defend herself, the strikes from this powerful man kept on impacting her. My father then reached for a branch on the ground, maybe his hands got tired, or maybe what I was thinking in that moment, *he's going to kill my mother.* My fear at that moment, started to turn to anger! I don't know why or how, but another being emerged inside of me, a spirit that now, after looking back at many moments in my life, only comes when in the worst situations. I started to pick up rocks from the ground, and without hesitation, I started to throw them at my father. One after the other, they started to sting him in multiple areas of his body. Suddenly, he was now being attacked. I don't know why the fear disappeared from me in the moment, but if it could save my mother, no matter what the consequences, I would endure it. My father, with the surprise attack of rocks being thrown at him, now had to defend himself and lost his focus on beating my mother.

President Barack Obama said in one of his speeches a long time ago, "In a child's life, they grow up to be one of two things, either just like their father, or the exact opposite." At five years old, I made the choice to be the exact opposite.

At a blink he rushed toward me to lessen the sting of the rocks and began beating me for my disrespect for hitting him. In the end, every strike that he gave me was worth any amount of money in the world. My mother, beaten and bloody, was able to run to one of the neighbor's house for help and hid there until she knew our father left the house. Later that day, she came and got my sisters and I, packed up our stuff, and we left. We stayed at family and friends' houses until my Grandmother was able to find a way to get us to America. From that day on, I never saw my father again. I had nightmares about that night for a long time. I vowed to myself to kill him if he ever hurt my mother again. He died about ten years later. I spoke to him once on the phone, it was awkward, but even though I was still angry—he was still my father. I forgave him in my heart before he died because I learned that God forgives us every day, no matter what we do or how bad we are.

My name is Damean Adams. My Mother and my Grandmother where the two most influential women in my life growing up. After leaving Jamaica and arriving in America, we lived in the city of Mt. Vernon, New York. We lived with my Grandmother in her apartment.

My mother was a strong woman, when younger—not the affectionate type, strong belief in God, persistent, hard worker, she made sacrifices to make sure that we would survive, she was not a person to complain and had minimum education but pursued and achieved her GED. She would say 'good job, son,' and that was all I needed to hear. My mother's punches where like George Foreman—heavy and powerful, she helped me win a lot of fights because many times, her strikes where harder than the people I was fighting. She overcame domestic abuse, left the abuse, and protected her children. She made sure I went to church and put God first

My Grandmother is wise, one of the best cooks in the world, she gave me my first fighting lesson, taught me how to never give up and to pursue my dreams. She taught me how to cook, her hands were faster than Bruce Lee if she had to slap you, always proud, and bragged about her grandson

I was an angry kid growing up, and I never understood why until now. After experiencing my father almost killing my mother, I had no respect for men or authority. We didn't have a lot of money, so I wore hand me down clothes. When you are young and in school, kids are cruel, everything is about fashion and looks. What is now called bullying was a normal thing for me growing up. It first started out because of how I talk because I was from Jamaica—I couldn't pronounce certain words properly. I would count one, two, tree, instead of three. My mother could only afford to buy payless shoes. My skin was darker than most, and I once thought girls don't like dark skinned guys. Then they made fun of my big lips, and that was the last straw. I started to fight back after that. I couldn't do anything about the clothes, my accent, my skin color, but I could definitely give them big lips like me after punching them in theirs. I'm not a violent man, but a kid can only take so much.

I was around gangs, drugs, guns, and for some strange reason, I didn't want to be mixed up in them. The fear of my mother was more than enough at that time not to. I remember I won a fight against this one older kid who kept bullying me. I thought the fight was over until he brought his bigger gang friends to me one day after school. They said fight him again, and they wouldn't jump in, if you have any street smarts, you'd know that was a set up for a beat down. One of them punched me in the face, I didn't go down because at this time, I knew how to take a punch. The oldest one started to lift up his shirt, and my eyes got big, shocked, and alert, to see he had a gun. Was this going to be the last day of my life? I had one of those single strap backpacks at the time. I grabbed the strap with my left hand, and lunged foreword as if I was going to punch the one with the gun with my left hand. He flinched to not get hit, and in that moment, there was a little gap of daylight for me to escape. I ran, I ran like I'd never run before because my life depended on it! Fear does something to you for good, especially when you need it the most. I ran through the school and off to another street, hoping, and praying that they didn't catch me. I got on one street, and there was this man who said, "Hey! I saw what happened, let me walk you home so that they don't do anything to you." He did walk me home, and at that moment, they didn't follow. The strange part about this moment however is, to this day, I don't know how he could have seen what had happened because it was on a different street. Also, no matter how hard I tried, from that day on, I could never remember who that man was, or what he looked like!

I wanted revenge, and I knew who to call to get it. Thank God we didn't find them, or else I probably wouldn't be here now. I started carrying a kitchen knife wrapped in foil paper to school for my protection in case I ran across them again. I learned how to vary my routes, and not be predictable. The hard part, however, was one month later, a good friend of mine fought the same guy. They saw him walking his girlfriend home late one night and put two rounds in his chest, killing him on the spot. He didn't have a chance to run his race! I kept all of these things from my mother and my family until now, I was afraid for their life.

Deep down, I always wanted better in life. I didn't want to struggle, and I wanted to do more for my family. It didn't matter that my Mother wasn't an affectionate person, I knew that she loved me. I wanted to make a difference and provide a better life for her. Track and field was going to be my way out of New York, I wanted to be the fastest man in the world and go to the Olympics.

Honorable mention—two men who early in my life helped show me hard work, Mr. Leonard Khan, the man my mother married a few years later. He showed me how to work for everything that you want in life, (May God rest his soul). And Coach Donny Dendy, a man who took me under his wing, treated me like son, and showed me how hustle and outwork everyone else in my way, (May God rest his soul). When coach Dendy told my mother about a scholarship to run at the Boys and Girls Club for the summer, that was all he had to say. My mother always wanted the best for me. I went undefeated that year in my age group. The next year, I lost one race against an African kid, I went to the only person I knew who could give me the confidence and inspiration to beat him—my Granny! She didn't have to say much to inspire me, simple but powerful words (train harder, don't give up, and go beat the African kid). She always brought the fighter out in me, and I did beat the kid. I started running varsity track and field when I was in middle school. I thought at that time that I was invincible.

Even though my mother was never able to see me run, she was always proud to see the medals I would win. Someone had to pay the bills, and at that time, she was the only one able to do it. I got injured my freshman and sophomore years, first my back, and then my hamstring. Long story short, the Olympics dream went down the drain. The worst moment in my life at that time, because I knew God gave me a gift of speed, and then it was gone. It was supposed to be my way out, the way I would provide for my Mother.

Depressed, my grades dropped, I barely graduated, and I didn't want to go to college unless I was running, and so that wasn't an option. I loved to cook but didn't get a response back from the cooking schools until it was too late.

I became one of the few, a United States Marine. I served my country honorably for eight years. My mother was scared at first, especially when we went to war, but she was proud, and that's all that mattered.

One of the greatest gifts that both my Mother and Grandmother directed me toward was God. No matter what

I did bad, or how angry I was at men and the world, for some odd reason, I knew I wasn't alone. I didn't have my biological Father to teach and lead me, so I learned to build that relationship with God. Then God started putting me in places, in front of people and experiences, to be who I am today. If it wasn't for my Mother and Grandmother who God gave me first though, I know I still would have had a relationship with God, but at a great cost and plenty more hard lessons and mistakes in life.

My Grandmother taught me:

- How to love, by showing it to me everyday
- She gave me my first fighting lesson in order to defend myself.
- She taught me how to love cooking, because it was an expression of love for the ones you are cooking for.
- My Grandmother taught me to respect everyone, and never judge a book by its cover. (She was older, but not slow, I disrespected her one day, and before I knew what happened, I was seeing stars, ear ringing—she was so fast, I didn't even see her move.
- My Granny also taught me that manners will carry you through the world.
- She also said, "Damean, in life, you must first kiss ass before you can kick it. In translation, she taught me that I had to learn the game by being a good follower, learn all the rules, practice hard, and master them, before I learned to bend them to my will.

My Mother taught me:
- Sacrifice is necessary in order to raise a family
- She taught me by her actions that you can't sit around and cry over one mistake. Life goes on, and you have to go with it.
- My mother taught me how to take a punch—when I was out of line, she made sure to straighten me back out.
- Mom taught me how to survive, that no matter what, or how little resources you have, you can make something out of it.
- She would tell me I can do anything I want to do, and I believed her.
- My Mother taught me through her actions to pursue goals, no matter how small or big—where there is a will, there is a way.

Because of my Mother and my Grandmother always pushing me forward, I won multiple races in my life.
- I didn't end up being the typical statistic.
- I graduated high school, something small, but what some of my peers never did.
- I became a United States Marine and served my country when it needed me the most. The only person in my family to join the armed forces at the time.
- I achieved my Associates degree.
- Authored and published a book before I was thirty years old
- I started a successful business, helping, and making people happy with our products.
- I Bought a home for my family to live in.
- I am a proud father of two amazing boys.

- God is number one in my life, and always will be.
- I'm still running to win other races in life, and I'll never stop running until I die.

To my Mom and Granny, thank you! Thank you for doing the best with what you had. Thank you for doing your best with where we were. Thank you for doing your best with who I was. Thank you for never giving up on me, especially during the times when the dark clouds where over my head. You both stared me to the greatest gift ever, Jesus Christ! Without Him, you know, and I know, I wouldn't be possible. Nothing was ever perfect, but you both taught me the most perfect thing— love God with all my heart and soul!

Mom, you were tough, but always fair. You protected me without me knowing. You cared for me without tiring. No matter how many shifts of work you had to do, you made sure I had a meal to eat. You loved without saying a word because you proved it every day by your actions—they spoke for you. I'm sorry that my father ever put his hands on you when I was a child. I'm sorry that I was angry at you without even know- ing it. I'm sorry because you had to take on the role of mother and father, in order to raise me. I understand now that you are a warrior, a fighter who never gives up and never leaves your team behind. Your actions throughout your life have been the greatest example of a hero that any child could ever need. These days, after having kids of my own, you have shown and con- tinue to show more love and affection that I ever experienced from you. Every year, I've watched you transform into the most wonderful mother, and grandmother—constantly praying, caring, and always making sure that we know we are loved and cared for. Thank God, and thank you from the bottom of my heart for being my mom. I love you always, your baby boy!

Granny, you are the foundation of our family. You are the only grandparent I ever knew, and God knew that you were the only one I needed to have! Thank you for teaching me humility. Thank you for giving me the love to open up my heart to have sympathy for others. Thank you for the many lessons in life that made me work harder than everyone around me. Thank you for encouraging me to achieve more than what anyone else could see. When you bragged about me, it inspired me to do more amazing things for you to be proud of. I was selfish before because I didn't want anyone else to know what an amazing Grandmother you are. Today, my secret is out. With all honesty, my life would be missing a part of it if not for you being in it. I love you from the bottom of my heart. I thank God every day for Him giving you time to see the man that you helped mold. I'll always and forever be grateful for you. Your Grandson!

CHAPTER 2

Destiny

Despite a picture-perfect upbringing with loving parents, financial stability, popularity, and emotional support all around, I found myself falling further and further into a world of chaos. Chaos riddled with drugs, sex, crime, and evil. At eighteen years old, I watched as the local cops who had known me my entire life put handcuffs on my boyfriend. I'd thought he hung the moon! Fourteen years older than me, the center of the party, and always had some type of illegal substance in his pocket. Little did I know, he was selling cocaine, and the police had been watching his every move, moves that often blindly involved me. By nineteen, I found out I was pregnant. A baby-faced teen who had just finished high school with honors as Salutatorian had been leading a secret life of drug abuse. How did I get here? I had dreams of becoming a doctor or nurse, and I watched as those faded, quickly replaced by fears of how I would raise a child when I was still a child myself.

My name is Amber, and this is my story. The story of how I won my race in the shoes of many souls.

Growing up, I thought the world of my uncle Dana, a small-town physician who served the people of our community for twenty-seven years. He delivered many babies, healed the sick, and helped many people manage their illnesses in order to lead a better quality of life. I couldn't go anywhere without someone asking if I was related to him. He genially cared about people, and, despite his own battles, was always eager to help others. I always dreamed of being the next generation of doctor in my family to serve my community. But I quickly realized that I had made choices that would alter that path.

By the age of twenty, I was married to the same man who couldn't seem to escape a life of drugs, mother to a 9-month-old, and pregnant with another. I had dropped out of nursing school and quit my job as an EKG technician in the local Intensive Care Unit, only to find myself feeling desperately alone in that 2-bedroom, run down mobile home in a town where I knew no one. I wasn't ready to admit defeat. I still wanted to chase my dreams; I still wanted a brighter future! When my oldest daughter was a year and four days old, my second daughter, Destiney, was born. With the most contagious smile I had ever seen, she completely changed my path, she changed my destiny!

Destiney's chapter in my story would soon be realized to be that which re-wrote the following ones. Soon after her birth, we learned that she was not like her sister, she would never do the things other normal children would. I found my world completely revolving around being her caretaker. Between tube feeding her through her J-port, meeting with the physical

13

therapist to work her non-developing muscles, cleaning her tracheostomy tube, all while also chasing a fully normal toddler around, I soon forgot any past desire of anything but being a caregiver for my children. And on June 29, 2006, my whole world would come crashing down! My Destiney could not stay; her work on this earth was done.

The following year after her death is still a blur. I knew I had to change everything if there was any hope of a brighter future for me and my surviving daughter. My marriage understandably failed, and returning home, to the one place that was always filled with people who loved and cared for me, seemed like the only option. Home, a word that is independently defined not by the amount of time spent there, but by the endless nurturing growth promoted from within. My parents never left my side. Despite my faults, mistakes, the drug use, the poor choices, the destructive behavior—they remained my biggest cheerleaders.

So, what now, what was I supposed to do? No career, a failed marriage, lost ambition, and a toddler to care for. I got back up! While relationships came and went over the years, my drive to have a career never wavered. I had always admired my father's service in the United States Army as a Medivac, and I aspired to do something to make him proud. I contemplated joining myself, following in his footsteps, serving my country, but that would mean leaving my daughter with the same man who was still selling drugs all these years later. That was not a choice I was willing to make. By this time, I had remarried, only to find I had chosen another chapter with a man who would never support my growth. He constantly enforced in me that I would never accomplish my dreams, that I couldn't do this or couldn't do that. He was adamant that women, especially me, did not belong in a field of service to the community that was deemed honorable. But I knew I had to choose my destiny—I was in control of my direction.

When I told my family and friends that I had drained my savings account to pay for law enforcement school, I remember feeling like I had something to prove. Many of them expressed their thoughts of how I would fail, how I wasn't right for that career, how my past choices would never let me accomplish this goal. But there, in the quiet corners of my life, remained my parents. No matter which direction I had ever chosen in my life, a turn to the right, left, front, or back... I found them there waiting, lovingly, in the corners. They expressed their fears for my safety but also reminded me whose daughter I was. They reminded me that I was more than my mistakes, stronger than my hurt, and capable of doing anything. My Daddy would always say "Can't never could!" as a reminder that if you think you can't; you won't!

I finished the law enforcement academy with the top defensive tactics award and went on to be hired in my hometown, one of the proudest moments of my life. I have been able to serve my community for over ten years now, going on to become the only female Deputy Chief ever in the history of my city. While I set out to follow in my uncle's shoes as a doctor, then my father's shoes as soldier, I found myself in another uncles' shoes as a police officer. But do we really win the race in the lone pair of shoes from one influence? I have learned that I won the race of my life in the shoes of many souls, and for every one of them, I will be eternally grateful.

To my amazing parents, thank you for never giving up on me. Thank you for knowing that despite the many times I have fallen, I would always find the strength to get back up. You have always reminded me that I am bigger than any problem, stronger than any hurt, and wiser than any obstacle. Because of your never wavering example of strength, love, compassion, and perseverance, I have chosen to never give up, to always keep striving for growth; spiritually, physically, and financially. I will go on to leave unforgettable shoes for my daughter to win her race in, all because you showed me how to win my race in the shoes of many souls.

Author's Notes,

Sometimes the most devastating things that happens to us in our life, we may think it happens *to* us, but in actuality; it happens *for* us. We may not see it right away, but eventually, it will reveal itself.

> *"You never know how strong you are,*
> *until strong is your only choice."*
> *~Bob Marley*

To get through the tough and darkest times in life, it takes tremendous strength; that many of us never knew we had! To continue moving forward with a positive attitude and a never giving up mindset takes an even stronger person.

The memories of our past will sometimes bring tears to our eyes and the feeling of loss. However, it's those special moments that we'll always be grateful for. The moments when we remember a certain sparkle in someone's eyes, their smile, the warm and comforting hugs, and the words that sometimes were never spoken, but you felt them in your heart, and it spoke to you deep down in your soul, loud and clear—I LOVE YOU!

Our race continues no matter what we may face in life! God has always been with us every step of the way. In the good times and the bad, in the lows and the highs, whether He spoke to you through a sign or the words from someone He sent to you in the perfect moment to comfort you with words of encouragement and support. He is always with us!

CHAPTER 3

Choosing a Different Path

I Won the race in my mother's shoes.

As the police officer continued to kneel on George Floyd's neck, and hearing a dying man cry out for his mother, I could not help putting myself in his position, and at that very moment looking for my mother for comfort. Like some of us, our mothers are the most instrumental person in our lives. She made the ultimate sacrifices to feed, protect, and nurture us. Coupled with the fact that my mother survived an abusive relationship and raised us by herself, it is even harder to digest.

Growing up, it was not uncommon for an unruly child to get a good butt whooping to get in line, but at the age of seven, that perspective changed late one night, being awoken by screams when I witnessed my mother being beaten with a serpentine belt by my father. With every lash on her back, she yelled out a painful cry, and I could only watch in horror. Frozen with anger and disgust, the rage in me wanted to protect her, but as a boy, like a helpless fawn, I could not do anything.

That morning I woke to find my mother in an abandoned shop across the street from our house. She lay on her stomach on the wooden floor on a cardboard piece with her back exposed, revealing every wound from the rubber belt that laced across her back. Having watched the movie *Roots*, her back looked like the slave character beaten by a jealous slave master, as if she had defied his every command. As I approached her softly, I was mortified to witness her like that; she only nudged a little to acknowledge my presence. Wanting to nurse her back to health, I was able to stumble upon a bottle of Jamaican White Rum. Without even thinking, I poured it on her back. With a grizzly scream, she yelled out, twisting and turning on the floor; I thought that I had killed her for sure.

A few minutes after the pain wore off, she turned to assure me she was okay. Feeling remorseful, I apologized for hurting her and not helping her that night of the beating. "If only I were a little bit older," I whispered to her as she turned to me and smiled. In a moment of tranquility, with the shop's back door open, we both lay on the floor, looking out the door at the gentle breeze that blew by.

A quote from the late rapper Tupac Shakur rings close to my heart, "A man that doesn't respect his mother will never respect his wife." Having witnessed what my father had done to my mother, I could not help but wonder what his relationship was to his mother. So, when a man lays hands on a woman or calls women bitches and hoes, it is damaging to my heart. Tupac once said, "**Since we all came from a woman**, got our name from a woman, and our game from a woman. I wonder why we take from women, why we rape our women, do we hate our women?" I guess they didn't have the type of mother I have!

My name is Chris P, and this is how I won the races In my mother's shoes.

I do not recall much of my childhood growing up in Jamaica, but I remember my mother's unconditional love in caring for my four siblings and myself, regardless of her emotional and physical pains.

I recall the small grocery store we owned, having few items on the shelves, to later have multiple stock products. I watched the hard work and dedication in making sure each shelf was fully stocked. Now and then, she would remind us of how my younger brother and I would go into the store and raid the shelves by taking a few sodas and canned sausages, consuming them and later filling the empty containers with water and placing them back on the shelves. And whenever she reminds me of that story, with a warm look into her eyes, she would smile and say "I would never get mad at you guys; I was more so happy that you guys were not hungry."

But life was not always so fantastic; it was not until Hurricane Gilbert devastated Jamaica that we felt hard times. With the store inventory nearly depleted, no electricity, no running water, things grew difficult, but my mother would strive against the odds to ensure that she cared for us. With the challenges and dwindling opportunities we faced, she decided to move to New York to live with my grandmother and later petition my siblings and myself to come live with her.

It is said that a Jamaican has over three jobs; my mother was that stereotype. Her schedule would consist of 8 a.m. to 10 a.m. as a home health aide, 10:30 a.m. to 1:30 p.m. as a server at the hotel, from 3 p.m. to 11 p.m. as a nurse's assistant at the hospital. In between the hotel and the hospital, my mother would find time to cook dinner and get ready for the next job. She would often complain about her aching feet, and seeing how hard she worked, we did not think twice about massaging them for her. To this day, I am still surprised at how she was able to work so hard and the fact that she was never fired for being always late.

Moving into a single-bedroom apartment in New Jersey, we quickly realized we did not escape the same hardship we faced in Jamaica. With five kids living in a single-bedroom apartment, it was not a comfortable arrangement. Even though it was not ideal, we were most grateful for having a roof over our heads and food in the refrigerator. But as time when by, things grew even more difficult for my mother in raising my older teenage brother. I remember being awoken one night with dishes thrown on the ground by my older brother and my mom yelling at him. Through the chaos, I found out that my older brother had been arrested for selling drugs. At the time, he'd thought it was an excellent way to help my mother pay for some of the bills, but that choice in life would later catch up with him.

As time went by, our living conditions improved from my mother's hard work; we went from a one-bedroom apartment to three bedrooms. It was at this point in life when my older brother's past caught up with him. With a duffle bag slung over his shoulder, I remember trying to escape to the bathroom where I thought my older brother would not find me crying. I was distraught by the thought of him leaving and serving a lengthy prison sentence. Not wanting to go without saying goodbye, he was able to block my path to the bathroom. Without saying a word, we hugged each other as if we were never going to see each other again; then I remember him telling me "Don't make the same mistakes I made." Shortly, I thought to myself, If I was that devasted with my brother leaving, I wonder the effect it had on my mother?

Seeing what happened to my older brother and not wanting to disappoint my mother, I started focusing extra hard on school and even getting a job working at the movie theater. I wanted to make something of myself that my mother would be proud of; I wanted to show her sacrifice was not in vain.

Without money, and a scholarship being nonexistent to go to college, and a career working at the movie theater was not the ideal vision for my future. I decided to enlist in the Marine Corps, hoping that would give me a fighting chance. Through the Marines, I was able to go to college, travel the world, get married, and start a catering business. I was able to grow a family and give them an experience I never had growing up.

For ten fruitful years of marriage, I thought I had made it. I lived the American dream; I had a well-paid job, house, car, motorcycle, and a business so that my wife did not have to work. But I later learned materialistic things were not the glue to keep a family together. It is the simple things such as I love you, thank you, how was your day, and many more. Over the years, I had taken those things for granted; things that caused us to grow apart. Suddenly, we were faced with the constant battle of divorce; just the thought of having our kids going through a broken home rendered me useless.

Dealing with my marriage's failure and my business that soon followed, I felt like giving up. At times, I found myself operating day to day in a mental fog. I was at rock bottom, filled with disappointment and failure. But through my mental haze, my mother was always there to pick me up and guide me through. I strongly recall a catering event when a customer became upset with the food and wanted a refund. To me, it was another failure that repurchased me into my mental haze. But like a patient guided into a counselor's office, I recall my mother pulling me to the side asking me, "If Jesus could not please the whole world, what makes you think you could? It is okay; you cannot please the world; you are going to have failures, but the biggest thing is to get up and keep trying."

I never did thank my mother for those inspirational words that day. Reflecting on her words made me feel rejuvenated; for I no longer aim to please the world but to show the world God's love. I could let go of things I could not control and work on the things that made me a better person. Thank you, Mom!

Author's Notes,

"Successful mothers are not the ones who have never struggled. They are the ones who never give up, despite the struggles."
                                                          ~Sharon Jaynes

When you have the example of a strong mother at home, choosing to be average in life should never be a question. Mothers are unique in so many ways, they have the ability to love you unconditionally like no one else can, unmatched only by God Himself! They also have an instinctive trait, determination, desire, and need to do whatever it takes to protect us against any thing or person that could potentially do us harm.

I believe that all mothers possess these superhuman powers within their blood and DNA. However, only a few of them use or summon these powers to serve them and their families.

"All that I am or hope to be I owe to my mother."
~Abraham Lincoln

As a boy growing up, we're always trying to find our place, show how tough we are, and trying to prove to everyone that we're capable. However, at the end of the day, all we truly want and desire is to make our mother proud.

Not having the influence of a father in any child's life can affect them negatively. The hard part about it is; even though we think it doesn't, at the root of the obstacles in our lives, it tends to have something to do with it. A mother will never really be able to take the role of the father, but when you have a strong mother, they become the best alternative.

"Each mistake teaches you something new about yourself.
There is no failure, remember, except in no longer
trying. It is the courage to continue that counts."
~Chris Bradford

Making bad decisions, and mistakes are a part of life, it's what you do afterward that counts. What we learn from life, from the hardest times that we face, are what truly defines our strength. These tough times make us tougher, wiser, and grateful to God that it wasn't worst. We must continue to look up, we must continue to move forward, we must have the attitude that failure is not an option. It's a choice, and it's not one that we will make or settle for, because God is with us always!

"The best way to make your dreams come true is to wake up."
~Muhammad Ali

CHAPTER 4

Through the Eyes of Another

Oh Paris! The city of lights and love...

Martin Luther King once said that *"nothing was more tragic than meeting a man breathless, lost in the labyrinth of life."*

That one morning of January 2011, I met him, sitting on a bench, his eyes utterly expressionless...

The winter of 2011 changed my life.

It just hit me! It was the first time I opened my eyes and realized that there was another world parallel to my life, another matrix called *"Street life."*

It all started when I met my homeless homie (as I used to call him) aka François X, the homeless guy from Châtelet les Halles...

He was hungry, he was cold, he was sad, or just deprived from his freedom and happiness, he was waiting, but waiting for what...? Just a blessed hand ...

I would like to dream without shame, that we all reach out our hand someday to someone who really needs it. And as

long as I'm dreaming, I'm only at the beginning, if I dream I can, and if I can then... I go on...

My name is Nadia Djebaili, founder of two organizations, and this is the story that made me who I am today.

I have a hard time talking about myself, even though I know that I can be proud of myself and of all the things I have achieved.

Of course, there were a lot of struggles and difficulties along the way. I failed at times and learned from those failures. Those failures helped me raise new standards. I knew what I wanted and what I didn't want anymore

Before meeting François, I was another person. Or let's say—I didn't realize what I had in me to be able to make little changes in the crazy world we live in.

I am a master graduate in foreign language. I have always been a big traveler and am very close to people. So, learning different languages made me realize during my travels that it was magic for a closer communication and fluid interactions.

I speak French, English, Dutch, and some Spanish, and I understand my tribe language. I am Berber from Algeria and was born and raised in France.

I had the chance to live in NYC for two years, London for two years, and Belgium most of my holidays. In my childhood, I spent time in a foster family (but only for holidays). At the time, my parents were struggling raising me and my four siblings. It was an occasion for us to travel, thanks to an organization for modest families that would send children away during vacation periods.

After my last expatriate trip in London, I came back to Paris in the middle of one of the coldest winters. And this is when I met François.

It's like God had put me in his way. I realized that day how grateful and thankful I was for all the good things that happened in my life. I was lucky to have a home to go to, to have my parents and my siblings, to have a job, to travel, to eat, to be clean... I realized that I was taking all of these things for granted... I cried that night. I don't think I had ever cried that much ever...

This is when I decided to change things. I felt an urge in me to help the needy, and moreover; I felt the urge to talk about it. To scream about it. To have everyone else see what I was seeing, feel what I was feeling, do what I would do.

It was hard at first to come to realize that not everyone is sensitive in helping other people. A real struggle for me. But I was patient, and I had to come to those people in a different way, in a smarter way...

I was on a mission. I felt it deeply.

Earlier, I was speaking about failure I have encountered.

Indeed, I had created an organization to help homeless people with my best friend at the time. Everything went well for seven years, until the needs got bigger, the events got bigger, and the team needed got bigger. This was great, but the bigger the team became, the further we were going from the vision I had...

Friendship and the good causes we could do started to change in a negative way as the organization got bigger. The more we are in a team the more difficult it is to manage a team and different characters.

It came to a point where after trying very hard to communicate with the new team for over two years—I am very patient---and trying to work together, it finally didn't work out. We were not on the same page. The events were, for some of them, more important than the actions toward the homeless themselves...

It was a hard decision that I took but I decided to give away this charity to my partner. 2018 was the worst year of my life. I had lost two friends from cancer, lost my best friend (arguments with the charity), and gave away my organization.

It was really though times, but if I had to do it all over again, I would!

I realized that I needed to sort out my surroundings. I stopped all activity for a few months, until I realized that I was made for this!

So, six months later, I created a new organization named Let's Dooo This! The best decision of my life! I was living and smiling again. I had cleared my environment of anything negative. I had lost a few friends in that process, but were they really friends then? And I have met amazing, supportive people. I have taken time to come a little closer to Allah.

I am proud that the first organization I created is still running today, and homeless people are still being taken care of.

I am proud to have upgraded by creating the new organization in my image:

Adding everyone's talent in order to achieve great solidarity projects.

I have learned to work with people differently and to know when to say no.

I won my race in the shoes of François. François is a small man, thin, frail, he wears glasses and has an unshaved gray beard. I would say he is forty-five years old, maybe a little younger, maybe a little older… They say he is too blunt, a little dumb. He doesn't speak much; he prefers to stay in his corner. Sometimes he pees on himself, yet I have tried many times to give him wipes and hygiene kits so that he can clean himself up, because there are no showers in the streets... he systematically refuses them. He renounced François, renounced his body, he divorced his body... His spirit lives in it, but refuses to be the roommate of this filthy body, which often smells like urine.

"They don't know," François said to me one day, "that living in the streets and being clean is a real challenge in my wandering situation. I respected myself before, I was handsome, I had dignity, I was clean… Anyway, just being in the street, I know very well that others think of me that I am dirty, poorly dressed, and that I smell bad. And then, I'm told to go see a doctor. To do what? So that he can make a strange face and hardly dare to touch me? Thank you, but no thank you…"

Just the evening before, François was in the emergency room, he fell and hurt his legs badly. He came out without any relief, not even pain killers since he had no insurance… his only relief was a pair of crutches that I kindly gave him a few days after... He was hardly consulted and had to walk for miles to get back to his new "urban shelter" ... Right there on the floor ...

François had his little habits, for four months, I saw him every Wednesday at the same spot, lying in his navy-blue duvet, on pieces of cardboard when they were not stolen. He was always the first one I saw, and he looked forward to the cupcakes, hot drinks, and meals that I could offer him. He always wanted black coffee with four sugars, no less, no matter my insistence of diabetic prevention!

He didn't speak much, despite the fact that he was not alone, behind him were crowded tents and people from all over Iran, Tunisia, Morocco, Afghanistan, Syria, Portugal, Australia, and even the great nation of France. They were around twenty, sometimes more, sometimes less.

Nobody bothered him, and their presence, although sometimes noisy or dangerous during the few fights that could occur, reassured him a little.

At least he had a place to stay, and it became his home. Plus, some organizations made food distributions during the week, he was grateful enough to receive hot meals almost every day when lucky, and the police station was right in front of him just in case... What else? Reassuring right?

Until one day, the same policemen he used to see every day threw all the tents and covers away, as if they were so easy to get hold of...

François came back to find his bed and urban housing wrecked and barricaded, there was no more access...

What was going to happen to him now? For once, he had found a safe place to hide. How was he going to survive? How was he going to be accepted by a group again? What upheavals in his routine!

He could no longer think, and his legs started shaking, and he fell on the floor again, overwhelmed by sadness, one more time his whole life fell apart... for once he had found quite a balance... Now what?

The next Wednesday, not finding them at our usual meeting place, I decided to take a walk around the block, and saw him...

He had no more place to sleep, no more sleeping bag, nothing mattered any more...

After giving him the oversized sweater I was wearing, I left him, with a big lump in my throat, trying to hide my tears... sad to be so helpless...

***

He was hungry, or he was cold. He was sad or just deprived of his joy. Free and locked up, he waited... for what? Just for an outstretched hand... And as long as I'm dreaming, I'm only at the beginning, if I dream I can, and if I can, then ... I go on...

He recognized me, he who had never said more than four words to me in four months ("Hello, thank you, or no thank you). He told me about his life. How everything fell apart from one day to another after he had lost his wife and kids in a car accident and couldn't cope with it. He started drinking to forget his pain, lost his job and got kicked out of his house because he couldn't pay the rent. He had a great finance job and had no money problem before this... His Friends and family disappeared little by little until he ended up all alone in the streets of Paris. He had lost all hope of happiness again and was just waiting for death to take him.

He explained to me that this could happen to anyone and not to take our comfortable life for granted. Then he smiled and told me that he would finally take the hygiene kit and try to fight for his life again. He had a beautiful smile, it was the first time I had noticed it! He also told me that my perseverance made him realize that some people cared, and it gave him confidence to rise up again.

At the end of our conversation, he even said that *"It could be worse!"* These words were so true and hit me badly! It was a heartbreaking and joyful moment at the same time... He finally opened himself to me, and more importantly... to life. And the more I saw him, the more motivated he was! Always smiling and giving me advice about my own life! It was a real slap in my face! We are always complaining about our lives, but, man... It could be so much worse...

I needed to do something!

So, I went to speak to some social helpers and gave him his location. I gave him a phone so that they could reach him.

Shortly after, they found him a social apartment

When the sun meets the rain, a miracle reveals thousands of colored drops in the guise of a rainbow, let me be one, me to ... just a tiny little sun drop ... to show to all that the storm knows how to smile! And as long as I'm dreaming, I'm only at the beginning, if I dream I can, and if I can, then ... I continue...

I think that François triggered something in me. He definitely opened my eyes on my own life. I realized that my life and my problems were minor. I looked at all the futilities and realized that I needed to change my behavior and stop complaining for silly things. Our daily problems (which dress should I buy, what should I eat today, oh this is not fancy enough, etc.) when you look at them, you realize how stupid you can be at times....

With experience, I also realized that we should not judge the people not willing to help other people. But if at least we can open their eyes and make them more sensitive to certain subjects by leading by example, it is already a step forward.

I got hooked in helping the needy people after that encounter and decided to start an organization.

People of all ages and from all walks of life may find themselves homeless for a wide variety of reasons (every homeless has his own story), and suddenly become reliant on various charities or the goodwill of people they meet along the way for shelter and survival. I wanted to support such people in trying to make a little change in their everyday life. I wanted to help our homeless homies and keep it within a warm family spirit. I wanted to raise awareness and open the eyes of the people so that they can at least see the homeless when they walk past them!

Because I didn't want to ask for money with a steel box at red lights or at the exit of a mall to ask people for a few generous coins, I decided to raise awareness in an interactive way by organizing concerts, stand-up comedy shows, sports events, in order to raise money in a cooler way. And I did!

This first charity is still ongoing It's been nine years now! I have given it to my former team, and today because of its success and of all the other organizations that I have met along the way, I have created a second charity in order to promote all the small organizations that are working in the shadow and are changing the world. I work with all kinds of organizations. In the last four years, I have organized solidarity events for different causes such as:

- Raising awareness on homelessness and doing a distribution
- Raising awareness on the discrimination against Albino people, especially in Africa
- Sending school items and clothing to Senegal
- Bringing Boxing gloves and hygiene kits to Cuba
- Raising awareness on breast cancer in Senegal
- Raising awareness on kids with mental health problems in Algeria and sending them materials to do some activities
- Helping an organization that is planting trees in Africa and raise environmental awareness
- And the latest project is working with a team of blind people and organizing a football tournament with them to show that they can still play some sports and have a social life

Like Mother Theresa, I think we live in a sea of poverty, but we can clean it up. Even if it's only a drop in a bucket, that drop is necessary ...
And if I'm dreaming, I'm only at the beginning, if I dream I can, and if I can... then... I go on...

Misery is a skyscraper, the top of which you will never see... But like Gandhi... "one step is enough for me," and if I am lucky enough to see a whole country walking behind me, perhaps, will I never know the result of what I have done, but if I don't, there never will be. And as long as I'm dreaming, I'm only at the beginning, if I dream I can, and if I can, then... I go on...

So, I thank you, François, and thank you, Allah, for having opened my eyes. Thanks to you, I see what is surrounding me, and I try to raise awareness on important causes.

By adding our talents, we can achieve amazing solidarity projects!

As long as WE are dreaming, WE are only at the beginning, if We are dreaming We can, and if We can, then... Let's go on...

Author's notes,
 "A person's most useful asset is not a head full of knowledge,
  but a heart full of love, an ear ready to listen
  and a hand willing to help others."
  ~Simple Reminders, Simplereminders.com

Sometimes the greatest joy and fulfillment in life is helping others! Having the ability to help someone who truly needs it sparks something amazing in you! Especially when you are doing it from the goodness of your heart and not just because someone is looking!

When you can learn and grow by being grateful for what you've already been given in life, it opens the door for you to receive so much more!

"Acknowledging the good that you already have in your life
is the foundation for all abundance."
~Eckhart Tolle

Everyone has a story in life, each story has a beginning, a middle, and an end. The most important part is the middle! It doesn't matter how you start your life, the end is inevitable, but the middle is where we leave our mark, where we make a difference, in our own lives and the lives of others! Yes, how you die can make a significant impact in a lot of ways, but I believe how we lived determines our peace when that time comes.

We live in such a busy world, we're always going and coming from somewhere, entering a problem or about to get over one. Often, we only focus on the things that are immediately in our lives, like our current situation, family, work, and for many of us, only what we see on the news. What we neglect to see, however, is everyone else. We pass and interact with so many people on a daily basis, but only enough for us to forget them in the next second when they aren't in front of us. We're mostly blind to what or whom is in front of us, even though we see them with our eyes, we truly don't see them, only what's on the surface, only what we perceive as our truth, not theirs.

"We are not here to judge people…
We exist to love, appreciate, and empathize.
Only when we understand that everyone has his own pains,
his own demons, his own tales."
~Swati Singh

We only have one chance at this thing we call life, finding out who we are, why we are, and what we're here to do are many times not the first thing on our list. Sadly, most people don't even put it on their list of things to think about. We all have untapped abilities in us that are waiting for us to unleash them and gift the world!

"The two most important days in your
life are the day you are born
and the day you find out why."
~Mark Twain"

Putting this book together has allowed me to see such beauty in people—and their lives! We all go through things in life that change us. We all have a cross to carry, we can't avoid that. I believe it's our small reminder of what Christ paid for us. Our cross keeps us humble, keeps us grounded, to know that life isn't perfect, to know that we all have to appreciate the opportunity that we've been given.

Many of us think we have the biggest cross to carry, and we believe others should recognize it and help us. However, if we can only stop for a second, and look around us, we'd be able to see that we aren't the only ones carrying a cross, and we definitely aren't carrying the biggest one.

For this to happen, we must first open our eye in our heart, to see beyond what's only on the surface. See the struggles that others are going through and be willing to understand that our lives could be much worse than what we believe it to be. To be willing to lend an ear to listen, a hand to pull someone up when they are down, and a shoulder for them to lean on before they fall. This is how I truly believe we can make one of our biggest impacts and difference in our lives, in the lives of others, in the world. It all starts with one word, the most important of them all. "LOVE."

CHAPTER 5

Second Chance of Life

My Grandmother who raised me died suddenly. So, from her death, I've always feared losing loved ones.

I'm Angela, and this is my story, my chapter. I won my race in the shoes of my grandmother and mother. My grandmother and mother were almost the same, they were both loving, kind, giving, and genuine people.

I started to go to the night clubs in high school, and my grades dropped. Eventually, I lost my focus to continue, and quit school. Two years after leaving school, I got pregnant and was tested positive for HIV. My baby girl was also born with the virus and lived only seven months before she passed. I got up from the fall.

I got pregnant again, and I knew the baby's life was more important than my own. I turned to God to clean up my life and give my life over to Him. With Prayer and hopes that my baby would be healthy.

During this time in my life, they did not have drugs to prevent HIV transmission from mother to child. By God's Grace and mercy, my daughter was born healthy, and HIV negative. My Mother prayed and probably fasted (Lol). She had the Faith that my baby would born completely healthy.

I kept moving forward past the obstacles, challenges, and defeats in my life. I have a beautiful twenty-five-year-old daughter, she's in college studying Biochemistry; my most precious Gift from God. I am a sales associate, and I see myself in the future owning several businesses.

My Mother would always say "be careful how you treat others, especially when you have children."

Thank you for loving me unconditionally and building good character within me. I thank God for blessing me with two of the most phenomenal and strongest women in my life—my grandmother and my mother. You've gone on, but you will always be a part of me, I LOVE YOU ALWAYS!

Author's notes,

"Being deeply loved by someone gives you strength,
while loving someone deeply gives you courage."
~Lao Tzu

It takes courage to love, knowing that at some point in our lives we are going to lose that special person. It takes courage to admit our faults, and most of all; it takes courage to share it with others!

We've all made many mistakes in life, and many of us have suffered or will suffer great consequences because of them. Doing what's right in the heat of a moment isn't always the most popular and favorable thing we choose to do. It's only when we get in trouble, get caught, or realize it's too late that we acknowledge we should've made a better decision for ourselves.

> *"If you do not change direction, you may*
> *end up where you are heading."*
> *~Lao Tzu*

Expressing defeat, fear, and our struggles in life takes strength, and only few have the courage to do it. However, change comes from learning the lessons that these bad decisions have taught us in our lives. It's applying them when we are face to face with temptation, again and again. We know deep down it's the same problem looking at us, but it now has a new face and a brighter smile, trying to convince us it's different.

> *"God, grant me the serenity to accept the things*
> *I cannot change, courage to change the things I*
> *can, and wisdom to know the difference."*
> *~Reinhold Niebuhr*

We must always remember; it's only when we think we can do it on our own that when we end up failing. Our truest strength comes from our God—He and He alone is our source of power to overcome any and all things.

*"God designed everything He created to be successful, a
bird that's meant to fly cannot succeed in a cage, a seed
that was meant to grow cannot succeed on the counter.
Life outside your ideal environment will destroy your potential,
because a wrong environment always means death."*
~Myles Munroe

CHAPTER 6

Grateful Rebellion

I was a very rebellious as a kid, I would never listen, and was suspended twice before high school, even before middle school. I was very hard-headed, and I did what I wanted. "Friend focused," as my dad would say, with no consideration of others and my future.

My name is Danielle S. M, or Dani, and this is my thank you letter, my story.

I'm winning the race in my mother's and my father's shoes. I'm still currently running the race, in their shoes, because I don't believe I'm done.

My mother is a God-fearing women, she's one of my best friends, she's brilliant minded, and so is my dad, in their beautiful unique ways that I truly admire and adore. My Dad is literally my hero, he's very wise beyond his years, he's very much like a bear, I would say. Hard core but soft when he needs to be. In school, I set my mind up, probably at a young age, not to succeed. I would aim low so that the expectations of others would not expect more out of me.

I was a C average student growing up and very loud and just annoying. I wasn't very focused. It was boys and friends all the time with me. It was only around my junior year of high school, when I was starting to prepare for college and adult life, that I began to focus more on bettering myself rather than just being average.

I aimed big and wanted bigger. Still being young, I didn't really know how to reach that goal. I definitely started shifting, and a better path was starting to be laid out for me. I wasn't ever into drugs or drinking, but I definitely wanted my independence and freedom. I didn't want help from anyone. Not even my parents. I was very selfish, but also, in a crazy; way self-seeking!

It wasn't until after I got married where a lot of my strength came from my parents. I started reaching out more for support and repairing the bond that we had broken.

My friends started betraying me, and I found more emotional support from my mom. She had my back, even when she didn't know what was happening at first. TRUE FRIENDSHIP, genuine, she showed me that, with grace.

My marriage was ending, and I was scared, literally scared, I avoided telling them because, in my eyes I was a failure, but my father was very supportive. My Dad was there for me regardless, I realized more how he has always picked me up even when I feel like I've been beaten. He never fails to make me feel special; when I feel like I won't ever be loved, he lets me know it. I find that quality in my Dad heroic.

I'm now enlisted in the Air Force and leaving soon for basic training. I'm beyond thrilled, I found more of myself than I could've ever imagine with the help of their guidance. I am also very happy, and I genuinely love my life.

My mom and dad always said; "Friends second, friends aren't everything, boys second, they will always be there."

I never understood that until I was an adult. Finding myself had truly changed my view of life, and as I continue every day, it's truly amazing.

Mom, Dad, I feel like thanking you is definitely too little, so small for all the patience, prayers, and guidance you have given me. I hope I make you proud, because I truly want you to know all of it paid off. I love you. This is only the beginning.

Author's notes,

> "The man who says he can and the man
> who says he can't, are both correct."
> ~ Confucius

When we set limitations in our lives, they tend be the only thing that we are committed to. Thinking negatively is easy, it seems like it's natural to us in a way. We don't have to work too hard to achieve less; for some of us, it's the only thing we've ever succeeded in.

> "Do not be conformed to this world, but be
> transformed by the renewal of your mind,
> that by testing you may discern what is the will of God,
> what is good and acceptable and perfect."
> Romans 12:2, English standard version

It's so easy these days to be caught up into what everyone else is doing. A good majority of the people in the world are allowing social media, friends, celebrities, and culture to create their identity. When this happens, we end up as copies of everyone else, and now we're predictable, another clone just like the rest. This is why so many people are controlled, and don't even know it!

> *"Honor your father and your mother,*
> *so that you may live long in the land the*
> *LORD your GOD is giving you."*
> *Exodus 20:12 NIV*

It's so important for us to remember where, and especially whom, we came through. Because of our parents, good or bad, they were chosen to bring you into this world. God chose them for a reason, beyond our understanding, because there was something in each of them that He wanted you to possess. In knowing this, they should be honored, by us acknowledging them, because God is never wrong.

We all know that not all parents are created equal. Some are good and some are downright terrible. Some love us, care for us, and some hate, abuse, and leave us searching for a missing part of our life's puzzle. As hard as it is to imagine when you've had a bad parent, they may not have had a good one either. Now, all of their parents' sins fall from them onto you.

We can be the change that we want in life, we can be the change that life needs us to be. We can change for the better, and when it's our time, if God wills it for us to be parents, the example that we give our children to pass on to theirs will be ones filled with love, understanding, forgiveness, and all of the traits that we know and wish our parents gave to us.

CHAPTER 7

Seeking Guidance

A situation that changed me was seeing a young kid get killed on the pavement. This young kid was someone who grew up under me. I saw him get through hundreds of obstacles in his life. When I saw him get killed, it put a lot of things in perspective for me. It showed me a different side of the world.

My name is Darryln Johnson. II, and I am the owner of Steeze Marketing LLC. I was born and raised in Topeka, KS, but I made sure to go as far as possible from there after I graduated college. I ended up going to an HBCU, called Coppin State University. My dad is from Chicago, and my mom was born in Detroit, and we all agreed that I needed to be around my culture a bit more. I went there for one year, and then when my dad got out of jail, I moved closer that way, which took me from playing D1 to NAIA basketball due to an abrupt decision. I used my NAIA grind and went overseas to play basketball for a few years. When I was overseas, I started seeing that I averaged more than the people who always seemed to get a new contract. So, I dug into it, and what I found was the players who marketed themselves and branded themselves thrived the most, so that is why I started my grind! I wanted to have a brand that problem solved and helped people!

I won this race in the shoes of Eric Thomas for the mental elevation side. And I won this race in the shoes of my mother when it comes to life!

Eric Thomas is a powerful man of integrity who teaches; you have to do the work to be great. The things that I have learned from him and his camp is that you cannot rely on anyone else, you have to find a way to make it happen, even if that leaves you broke. The things I have learned from him I apply daily, and that's why my life and brand is elevating daily.

My mom is a powerful woman of God, and woman of integrity. She has taught me that being the person God intended me to be and not running from it will truly bless me in the long run. She has also encouraged me to be great. My mom is literally the Jordan of being a community and church activist, and I am here for it daily!

I fell down the wrong path between 18–23. It wasn't like I was in trouble with the law or anything of that nature, but I started trying to be like everyone else! I went away from my personal morals, ethics, and general discernment's. Unfortunately, this had me thinking like everyone else as well. Partying was high on the list, after basketball of course. Girls were on that list right after that. It was just a life of repetitive nothingness in my opinion. I feel as though I was born to be great! I was born to move mountains! God has intended me to be something great, and I failed to follow His timing and His word.

I got up from this fall when I realized that my life did not look like it should. I had a college degree and a professional overseas resume, and I was still standing still because of my mindset that "The world owed me." In my opinion, I thought that I would become a statistic if I didn't change what I did! I was tired of playing the victim in every area of life, so I took a year and just isolated myself. Sometimes you have to isolate to elevate in life!

I won this race by the grace of God. After following what He laid out for me, I was able to elevate and grow to a point where I was able to quit my job and run my business full time! After winning that race, I'm looking to run thousands more before my time is done! My mother would always say "As a Black man, you have to make it happen. You cannot play the victim, because the world will use that against you." My Father gave me the gift of consistency. He made me shoot 100 shots after practice every day in HS, and Because of that consistency, I went D1. The best advice I ever got was "You have to isolate to elevate."

Momma, thank you. Thank you for teaching me how to be a man. Thank you for not handicapping me. Thank you for not letting me "Play the victim." Thank you for being MOM and DAD when you had to. Most of all; Thank you for being the woman of God that He intended you to be!

Author's notes,
> "Don't make a habit out of choosing what feels
> good over what's actually good for you."
> ~Eric Thomas

No matter how much we want to walk the straight path in life, something, someone, or situations tends to push us off it. We know better, but in the heat of the moment, the pleasure and adventure is more exciting than doing what's right.

*"You either do what is hard and succeed or do
what is easy and live in mediocrity."*
-Eric Thomas

The decision to look at our present situation and say to yourself that you're better than this is not an easy thing to do. It takes a strong person who has either reached the lowest of the low, had an awakening experience, or reflected on how and who raised them to be better.

*"Train up a child in the way he should go;
even when he is old, he will not depart from it."*
Bible, Proverbs 22:6 ESV

Parents may not see the results of the positive values that they instill in their children when they are young. They may not even see it when they veer off the path that we know they should walk. They may go down some ugly and dark roads first before it happens, but with God's grace, it will.

Our parents will teach us many things, and depending on the parent, they may be good or bad. Nonetheless, we will be taught them. Some of these things will teach us what to do and how to do them. If we are truly observant and understand the difference, we'll take the good, use it, and the bad; use it also... to know what not to do in the future.

> *"People with good intentions make promises,*
> *but people with good character keep them."*
> *-Eric Thomas*

CHAPTER 8

Choosing a better Path

My Mother left an abusive marriage, with two children with no family support system near her. This was such an example to me to never allow someone to treat me less than I deserve.

I am Ambra B, Life Coach and Aromatherapist. I definitely won my race in my mother's shoes. She has taught me about perseverance, trusting God, self-respect, and following your dreams.

I am writing about my mother. She had a very rough childhood and has overcome so very much in her life, which has inspired me in my journey.

I got into drinking and using drugs in my adolescence. My mother was very direct, blunt, and loving when she helped me to choose a better path of greatness. Her belief in me helped me to believe in myself and dig deep on why God has me on this earth—really uncovering my talents and spiritual gifts, helping me to have faith that my life has great purpose.

Coming from a background of poverty, my mother had seen a lot of disfunction, addiction, and trauma in her childhood. She helped my path by sharing her love and wisdom of God, faith, hope, and love. That no matter what happens or how hard things get, we can always start over and choose to live in joy. I started to have faith in myself and my future. I started praying regularly and reading my bible. I began to think of why I am here and what God's plan was for me. I started making goals and educating myself. I invested in myself. I started my own business and am helping others live happier healthier lives through it.

About five years ago, I started my own business; I have become a certified life coach and licensed aromatherapist. I am a successful work from home momma of two littles. I serve clients all over the globe and have had the privilege to speak at events to hundreds of people, encouraging them to pursue their passion and purpose. I help others to break through limiting beliefs that may be holding them back. I am now a successful Entrepreneur, building a legacy for my family. My dream is to buy my mother a house and take care of her, since she took such great care of me.

My mother would always say, God has a plan for your life. You have to trust and have faith; you must always treat others as you want to be treated; You are capable of anything!! The only thing standing in your way is the faith to believe it is possible. All you need is faith the size of a mustard seed and God will use it!

Dear, Mom,
I am so thankful and grateful that God chose you to be my Mother. Everything I have ever needed in a mom, you have gone above and beyond in every way. You are the most kind, compassionate, generous person I know.

You have been there for me when I had no one. You have picked me up and kept me going in my darkest days and celebrated the most joyous moments of my life. You have taught me about hard work, faithfulness, understanding, and loyalty. You taught me how to be a lady with passion and purpose for her divine mission. You never ever give up, and because of that, neither will I. Because of you, I am able to pass all of these qualities on to my own children. I am living my dream life because of your support, love, and encouragement. I will forever be grateful for you sharing Jesus with me and instilling faith in my heart. I love you to the moon and back, forever and ever. I love you!!

Author's notes,

One of the greatest things that we can do for our children is to introduce them to their true creator!

> *"They come through you, but not for you."*
> *~Kahil Gibran*

Many times as parents, we believe that we must control everything that our children do. We sometimes believe that we alone know what's best for them, and they aren't capable of making their own decisions.

In so many ways, almost any parent can justify moments where we truly believe this. However, I truly believe that as parents, God has entrusted us with a great responsibility to take care, love, teach, and guide our children only until they reach the age of adulthood.

I'm not saying give up all responsibility and stop caring after that point in their lives. What I mean is; parent at a great distance. You can never be the master of your life if your teacher is always telling you what to do and is not satisfied because you didn't do it their way!

> *"Give a man a fish, and you feed him for a day.*
> *Teach him how to fish, and you feed him for lifetime."*
> *~ Lao Tzu*

As parents, it's our duty to teach, empower, and encourage our children to be better than us. Each generation should learn to be better than the last, because we should teach our children to learn from our mistakes. We can impower them with the knowledge that we wish we knew when we were their age. We often tell ourselves when we reflect on our past *"If I only knew then, what I know now, my life would be so different."*

I'm not saying children won't make mistakes or go down some of the wrong paths in life! They too must learn from their own experiences in life, because that is and always will be one of their greatest teachers! However, because you first led them down the path to seek God first, they will always have the opportunity to turn into the light, away from the darkness! You'll have given them the greatest of all gifts; "LOVE."

"Love is patient, love is kind. It does not envy, it does not boast, it is not proud. It does not dishonor others, it is not self-seeking, it is not easily angered, it keeps no record of wrongs."
1 Corinthians 13:4-5

CHAPTER 9

Searching for Truth

Thank you, Father.

I have been blessed with several influencers who showed up at critical times to guide my mind and help form my perception of who I am in the world and how I relate to external systems and norms.

I was born in the capital city of Ghana, and the omnipresent force that guided everyday living was religion. My family was especially exposed to Christianity and the various denominations that flooded the continent. For starters, my mother was a member of the Evangelical Presbyterian Church, an institution in Ghana, which will further segment into two factions during my formative years. My Grandfather had essentially founded the branch of the church in the Volta region of Ghana and was a prominent leader.

My first church was a Baptist church, located directly across the street from my childhood home. They flooded my young mind with many bible stories which spanned Joseph in Egypt, Mosses and the commandments, Joshua and the wars, David and goliath, to Jesus and his teachings. By my teenage years, I had read the King James version of the bible at least one time cover to cover. By the time I turned thirteen, my father was a significant part of life again, and as the universe would have it, he was a protestant Christian. I switched churches and took on their teachings, noting the subtle differences. Their focus was the new testament, praying in tongues, and miracles. No need to focus on the old testament, Christ had fulfilled the law and we were living in a dispensation of grace.

Needless to say, they all had Christ as the savior and emphasized the looming threat of hell for those resistant to Christ and his teaching. I was aware at that age that the bible mentioned *'thou shalt not fear'* at least 365 time in the King James Version of the bible but I remained terrified of hell and the many things I seemingly did daily to earn my ticket there. Additionally, I was told applying critical thinking or worldly thinking to church or bible was tantamount to blasphemy, a sure way to end up in hell.

The idea that the bible was a complete and sacred text that could not be amended was something I was keenly aware of by the time I was sixteen. My parents finalized their divorce around this time, and I was shipped off to a Catholic junior seminary and boarding school. It wasn't long before my youth pastor in the protestant church exposed a deep fissure between the protestant community and catholic faith. Essentially, he was of the notion Catholics were Christians, and he admonished me to be aware of their teaching. Once I got to the junior seminary, I learned the catholic bible had additional books that were not in the King James version I had thoroughly consumed.

By end of my first semester break, I was loaded with questions. Who had the earliest version of the bible? How were the books chosen and compiled and for what purpose? Did the catholic faith add to the bible or did the protestants take away from it? If so, who would face the damnation promised in revelation for adding or subtracting from the bible? If judgment day was a thing in the future, what happened to everyone who was dead now? How could Jews be guaranteed a place in heaven if they didn't believe in Christ but not the rest of us? Why was there discrimination in heaven? What did 666 mean and how would we know? I approached my youth pastor with these questions, and it became clear quickly he was not intellectually curious or informed about his chosen profession. He replied with the same canned answer "do not try to use your earthly mind to understand the things of God." That answer proved very unsatisfying at best.

I returned to the seminary with similar question for father Poku, his approach was wildly different, he explained the church's teachings about judgment day and the idea of purgatory and historical origins based on the need to raise money to build St. Peter's basilica and the politics that lead to the many denominations. I heard for the first time that Revelations could be a past event and there is significant evidence the antichrist was Caesar Nero. The hand of God is concealed and sometimes directed by the acts of men. He encouraged me to research and question everything.

Many years later, I will find myself in Afghanistan, fighting the war on terror or radical Islam, and wondering why the suicide bomber didn't question his religious philosophy. Why they believed what they believed and how it made sense. It was apparent to me that like many born into the Christian faith, they made no efforts to question their beliefs or its origins and were quick to dismiss the hand of man. They were victims of train the kids the way they should go in their religious beliefs and when they grow up, they will not depart from it, but instead, they will ensure their kids adopt it, even to their detriment, and beat them over their heads should they question it. I doubt that my conversation with the priest some twenty-four years was significant to father Poku, however; it changed the way I perceived the world and myself in it. I question everything and think deeply on the questions of government and religion. In the end, God is constant, all religion comes and goes, and none is spared the selfish human need for power and dominance. Thanks Father!

Author's notes,

"We are either in the process of resisting God's truth
or in the process of being shaped and molded by His truth."
~ Charles Stanley

When we're born, we become a blank canvas that people paint on without our permission. We're taught many things by our parents, teachers, society, television, just to name a few. With so much information, it becomes hard to know what is true or false.

I've come to realize that mankind is great at adapting to times and situations! I've also noticed that we're able to adapt things to fit our needs, want's, and desire's.

> *"The reasonable man adapts himself to the world; the unreasonable one persists to adapt the world to himself. Therefor, all progress depends on the unreasonable man."*
> ~ *George Bernard Shaw*

What we consider the truth is derived of what someone else tells us is the truth. Case in point, it takes a certain amount of times for a baby to hear their name before they respond to it. Once they hear it enough, they begin to understand, this is me. Now that they know their name, you can't tell them any different. We'll fight for our name, it becomes our identity, and forever a part of us. So this is the question; Is our name, who you are, or who someone told you that you are? When we continue to tell ourselves, or hear things consistently, it gets programed in us as the truth. I'm poor, I'm ugly, I'm a Ni%&&r, you know what I mean, I'm worthless, etc. These are only things that someone else tells us, but the TRUTH is—we don't have to accept them. We have within us the power to change our path and view, a power given to us by our creator!

> *Nothing of me is original. I am the combined effort of everyone I've ever known."*
> ~ *Chuck Polahniuk*

They're still so many things in this world and universe that man still can't explain, create, or duplicate. The truth, I believe, is in us, which is why we question things, why we create, why we discover, why we are instinctively curious!

We just have to ask the right question, and if and when God wants us to know that answer, it will be revealed to us. However, some people create their own hypotheses, and who am I to question them, as long as it doesn't lead others down the wrong path. I believe in God almighty, one of His many names! I believe in "Yeshua" Jesus Christ! Because God gave us the greatest gift with love; "Free Will," our ability to choose!

CHAPTER 10

The Betrayal

I won the race in the shoes of my parents.

I am Kimberly S. and this is my chapter.

I was Twenty-nine years old when I met the man who I married at thirty-one years old in 2001. I thought that it was time for me to be married. It was another thing to check off the list. I was a single mom with one son who was ten years old when I married. This was not the first man who asked me to be his wife. He was the first one who I married. My sisters jokingly gave me the nickname "ring girl" because I had acquired a few engagement rings. I asked all the right questions before I married. Do you smoke? Do you drink? Do you have children? Are you seeing anyone? Does anyone think they are your girl? Do you attend church regularly? I loved that man; we built a great life together.

Things started getting rocky.

I realized that he was a smoker. He'd lied and said he wasn't. He drank. A lot. Initially, it appeared that he was a social drinker. Looking at his parents and brother, I should have known that he was a heavy drinker because they all were. I hated driving at night when we would go out. I figured he'd not drink, so that was my saving grace. So, I thought. Eventually, I would learn that I needed to drive myself to certain places so I could leave early before he started acting a fool.

I should have left at year five.

When I asked him why he lied about all of the initial questions that I'd asked, his reply was: I knew that you wouldn't be with me, I had to lie.

Things weren't always bad. As we grew with each other, things looked better. No matter where we went, he was always the center of attention. He loved attention. Me, not so much, I was okay with blending in. I began hating to go out with him. We tried counseling, but we would argue after leaving. Then he decided that he didn't want to go anymore because everyone always saw things my way.

My mom moved in with us.

My mom's health took a drastic change for the worse. In an effort for me to not keep paying her bills and buying her groceries, she moved in with us. It was cheaper that way, and we had enough space. God gives you "stuff" so you can be a blessing to others. It was great having her with us, and she was a distraction from my marriage. My son loved having her around. He was spoiled by her. My mom and I would commute together to work. I was the driver. Now that I have my mom, my husband would find other things to do. My mom died in 2007, in her bedroom at my house, while I was in the hospital tending to my son. My husband was the one who found her. My mom told me a few times that she heard various conversations that my husband and I had and that she would not interject or offer her advice or opinion unless she was asked to do so by me. I never asked her to. Death has a way of bringing people closer. I thought things were getting better.

His uncle moved in with us.

The uncle was a drug user. My husband and his family thought it was a great idea to have him get away from country living for a while and stay with us. Not a good move. Things started disappearing from our home. A crack pipe was found in the room that he stayed in. He had to leave.

My son goes away to college.

Having my son out of the house meant we would be together more. That didn't happen, and things started looking bleak again. I was praying for a transformation and renewing of our minds. I was involved in church, community activities, and started a catering business. I was growing and doing everything that God placed on my heart to do. I had my husband's support, and yet, we still seemed very distant. I was beginning to think that something was really wrong and I didn't want to come to grips with it. My sister once told me that my dad asked her if everything was okay with me and my marriage. I actually blew up at her and told her to tell dad: if he wants to know something, tell him to ask me directly. I was hurt that someone could actually see that something was "wrong."

My dad got really sick suddenly.

When my dad took ill, my sister decided that she would have him move in with her—since I took care of my mom, she wanted to step up and take care of dad. I attended many doctor visits with him and even was the mediator when the two of them would have their many spats about what my dad should and shouldn't eat. My dad often offered bits of wisdom during our times together. I will forever member him reminding me that I don't need a man to do anything for me. I believe that this was my dad's way of letting me know that he knew that I was not happy with certain things in my marriage. My dad died in 2014 at his brothers' home while getting ready to go on a road trip. Again, death is that thing that brings people closer. Now, I am without both parents. My husband still has both of his parents, so it made all of us closer for a great while.

I was in remission from Crohn's Disease during most of our marriage. I would have the occasional stomach ache when I was stressed but nothing really major. My husband often told me that I was faking being sick so I wouldn't have to go places or do things.

I asked God to show me a sign.

One evening, after work, I had gotten home late. I was taking a CPR course in Washington, DC. I just knew that he would beat me home. Time went on, and finally after midnight, he arrived home. Drunk.

That's not the worst of it, he was talking to another woman via facetime, as if I wasn't there.

I will leave out all of the gritty details. I had asked God to show me a sign, and He did. If you aren't ready for God to do a work in your life, do not ask Him to show you anything! That night, I asked my husband to leave. He did, but I was sure he would come back. No, he had never hit me. Yet I believe emotional abuse is right up there with physical abuse. There were many occasions that my husband would tell me that he knew that I was afraid of what my family would think and therefore I would never leave him or get a divorce. I decided, to leave my home. I went to my sisters' home. I stayed there for a month or so. I eventually went back to my home after I realized that my husband had no intention of going back. He couldn't afford to live in the house and pay all the bills alone.

I filed for divorce the next year (at the time in Maryland you must file and wait a year), and it was granted in October 2016. I learned so much during my fifteen years of being married to him. I must say that I have absolutely no regrets.

Life goes on, Mom and Dad!

You both raised an educated, independent, and kind woman. Though you aren't here to see that I moved on with my life. I believe that your inner support and guidance to take the leap to move on was what pushed me. Why did I wait so long? Was I really afraid of what people thought? I am remarried and I know that you both would absolutely love this man. No, I did not look to get married again. I was okay focusing on myself and my newly single life, and God allowed my husband to find me. How did my wonderful husband of two years propose to me? I'm glad you asked! I was sick. I was experiencing a really bad Crohn's flare. A flare so bad that I was contemplating going to the ER. My husband sat on the bed and opened a box with a ring and said "let's do this." The day he proposed to me let me know that I was going to be okay.

Author's Notes,

> *"Oh, what a tangled web we weave…*
> *when first we practice to deceive."*
> *~ Walter Scott, Marmion*

One of the hardest things to deal with in life is the truth, especially when you thought you were already dealing with it.

It's always hard when we find out what we thought was true was really false. It hurts more when it's about person that we love. A fictional character playing a role in our story of life.

Sadly though, this isn't the only place that these types of things happen.

Deception is all around us, we're deceived on a daily basis. This deception can be in our home, office, society, government, and even our churches. It's not the institutions themselves, it's a small percentage of the people in them.

Not everyone that we meet will have our best intentions. Come to think of it, most people we meet will have the best intentions for themselves, and almost never think of you. It's necessary to know these things so that we can prepare for disappointments.

I'm not saying that we don't give people the benefit of being amazing, because the majority of people we attract could be just that. However, if we ever get disappointed, it's good to remember that we're all humans and never perfect.

> *"Your hardest times often lead to the greatest moments of your life.*
> *Keep going. Tough situations build strong people in the end."*
> *~ Roy T. Bennett*

Life will throw many things at us that we will never see coming. These things come in the form of the wrong people, loss, bad health, breakup, divorce, and death. Each of them will hurt, each of them will take time for us to process, learn, mourn, grow, forgive, and move on.

Things will not all ways be what we expected, and the people in our lives will not be in it forever. It's what we take away from these experiences with people and situations that make us better or worse because of them.

> *"You don't fear change. You fear the unknown. If you knew the future would be great, you'd welcome the change to get there. Well, the futures is great. Proceed."*
> *-Joe Vitale*

CHAPTER 11

It Takes a Village

The latest and most interesting thing that changed me was seeing how my Mother's health has changed but depleted after working so long and hard all of her life. My mother raised six kids after my father died but built a village around us with the help of her family and the spirit of my father's family not too far from us. Her health started a downward spiral after her body didn't want to do the same type of work and her body couldn't agree with what her mind wanted to do. Over the years, she was the first family to get diabetes. Ironically, I was already on a journey to eat healthy but needed a deeper vision. My outlook on the overall health of people has been something that changed on the components that work together.

I'm Johnny Dyson. MBA, and this is a short story of my new chapter on this old journey I've been traveling on.

I'm from a small city called Benton Harbor, MI where many famous people are from, but many don't know about it. A simple saying is, we're the most famous smallest city in Michigan. Every city in Michigan knows about Benton Harbor, but outside of the state you have to describe it being next to Notre Dame college.

My father died when I was eleven years old, so to say I wore one person's shoes would be remiss. I've been blessed to have the knowledge to learn from many people in my life, whether it be the big drug dealers, professional athletes, entertainers, friends, family members, or civil rights activists. Simply because I had to find the right journey that would lead me to being whoever I'm supposed to be, but supposed to be during certain times while I'm evolving on this journey. I'm made up of all of the people who have help me along my way. I can say I won my race with everyone who would lend me their shoes to run when I didn't have shoes of my own, because I struggled with the knowledge of how to maneuver through all of this information without having a guide, but still messing up at the same time.

I'm simply giving a humble ode to all of the people who have helped me find the right shoes that were meant for me. My family and friends have helped me, believe me, and give me the confidence that whatever I am, I'm good enough. Good enough to fail and get back up again, because I've already won just being me. I've learned directly and indirectly from family members and friends on what not to do, what to do, and most of all to sit and listen. I've been able to evaluate decisions on what is the best move to make based on the foundations of learning from others. My mother worked so much, we had to watch our younger siblings, but we had friends who would still come by our house and do what they can just so we can get by.

I've been blessed that many of my cousins are almost extended brothers and sisters and we grew up around each other all the time. I have an aunt who is like a sister, but another is like a mom. Many of my uncles are like brothers to me because I was molded on manhood from them. All of the women in my life have helped me to understand that they are the reason of my existence. I have an amazing wife by the name of Theresa who has challenged me to the point of submission of knowledge and learning there is more than one aspect of love, that evolves with you or without you.

I've fallen numerous times. After my father died, I didn't care about anything, but didn't know what was going on at the same time. My mother worked so much that she could only watch us so much, so we missed a lot of school. I was always told I was smart, so I kind of got by without trying. I had an administrator who wouldn't let me quit. Luckily, over the years, we would all climb out of it, then I was doing stupid stuff, stealing, was hanging with the wrong crowd, and went to juvenile a few weeks, and years later I started selling drugs and smoking weed. I didn't see a light at the end of the tunnel.

I was fortunate that I hung around my uncles and their friends. For some reason, they treated me like a brother, and while hanging with them, I sat back and looked at why are they were treating me like this, what is it about me, who am I, and more questions of where I stand. After I sat with those thoughts and reflected on some of their accomplishments, I had a daughter and knew I had to at least finish high school, but how can I do more than the average, cause I didn't see myself living in a small city. Although there is nothing wrong with living in a small city, I just knew I had dreams to do more with better resources and see what is out there. I stopped doing everything and finished school, but went a step further by going to college, getting a great job, and have been the talk of my family on what success is.

Although I still consider myself in a marathon on my journey, I've been awarded with the gratitude of inspiring many family members to go to school, raise a family, and believe in themselves. Out of my immediate family of siblings, I'm the only one to graduate high school. Out of a few generations of our family, I'm the only one to graduate from college, and I'm one of the few to have master's degree in business administration. I have an amazing family with my wife of twelve years married, but been together for twenty-four years, we have four kids and a grandchild, I'm currently taking care of my mother and mother in law. I'm currently building an empire of different businesses with family and friends, but the same people who have helped me along the way. I'm also a certified life and wellness coach, nutritionist, and fitness coach with the goals of helping people change their health over the next few years. My wife and I are Relationship Coaches with a podcast that helps people, but more importantly is helping many of our outreach inspirations.

I've gotten far by keeping in mind what I heard someone say years ago—it helps me on making calculated decisions. "You have two ears and one mouth." You must listen before you speak. Listening has been the thing that has led me to absorb information that comes from many walks of life and allows me to keep an open mind. Listening has also helped me in my new career but keeps feeding my curiosity on what level is next. While I thought I wasn't going to go back to school, I'm fortunate to continue to be a student of just learning whatever I can while I'm on this journey of evolving. I'm only as great as the things they've put in me, but was possibly passed to and through them. I've been blessed to have made it this far, but hopefully the people who have allowed me to stand on their shoulders so far will continue to hold me up to do many other great things.

I would like to thank my beautiful wife Theresa Dyson, my children (JoNeisha Dyson, Jaiyana Dyson, Johnny Dyson III, JaRiyah Dyson), grandchild (ren) Kayden Dyson, mother (Barbara Dyson), father (Johnny Dyson), grandmothers (Ruthie Green and Mary Lampkin), grandfathers (Johnnie Dyson, Eddie Green), my sisters and brothers (Percilla, LaQuilla, Eddie, JaVontae, DeVondre, and DeQuandre), all of my aunts (Pearlitha, Tiajuana, Linda, Joan), all of my uncles (Addison, Nate, Frank, Bruce, Daniel, Lee, Pinto-Michael), all of my cousins, nieces, nephews, all of my family, and a numerous amount friends.

Over the years, I've spent numerous amount of time with everyone, cultivating this thing called life, but being molded in the process. Fortunately, everyone has been an interesting part of my journey, to the point of me realizing what grace is. The knowledge I've gained from everyone was an interesting part in the essence of my growth. I can't just thank or say it's been one person, because the small community and city I lived in allowed everyone to chip in on my success. Everyone has taught me something that I either needed at that time or had to save it for later.

There is a definition of grace, but I'm not sure if the definition is worthy enough. I could complain about all of my hardships, what I didn't have, what was wrong with me, and more, but those are the things that have made me a different kind of diamond. I just needed that pressure to make me who I am. At least I had whatever I had that gave me the experience to a foundation of greatness. I'm excited at what lies ahead, and hopefully, everyone is appreciative and happy with where I'm going. Blessings!!!

Yours truly and deeply indebted,

Johnny Dyson. MBA

Author's Notes,

> *"Any man can be a father, but it takes*
> *someone special to be a Dad,"*
> *~Anne Geddes"*

It's rare to have a great Mom and a Great dad, but it's hard when you lose one of them too soon! Losing a parent is never an easy thing for anyone, but it's so much harder when you didn't have enough time to really know and learn all that you could from them! In many ways, it's an emotion of loss, and many times we go searching for a replacement of what we believe we need in other people.

> *"When you look into your mother's eyes,*
> *you know that is the purest love you can find on this earth."*
> *~Mitch Albom*

A mother's love to many of us is the warmest thought in the world! Life can be cold to us at times, especially as a child, but having a mother to care for you, when it seems no one else does, is the greatest blanket ever!

Finding a way to pay back our parents for the love, care, sacrifice, and dedication is sometimes the number one thing and purpose for striving to be better in life. To say thank you, to say I got you now, it's my turn!

> *"It takes a village to raise a child."*
> *~African proverb"*

Many times, we think of a child growing up with their mother and father as the most influential people in their lives. In some cases, it's absolutely true, in many cases, it's false, but there are few cases, a special selection of us, who live to witness and experience being raised by a community of people, not just our parents.

Our parents, in many cases, will play the biggest roles and influence, but when you have the support of others who care about you and your future, it becomes the greatest lessons that school could never teach you!

> *"If you are not willing to learn, no one can help you.*
> *If you are determined to learn, no one can stop you."*
> *~Kushandwizdom"*

The extended family, village, town, or communities in some places have close connections with everyone. Almost everyone knows who you are, who you are related to, and what you've done, and didn't do. The tradition and customs in certain tribes require and expect that family and community take care of their own.

This type of honor system, if followed, builds confidence and accountability into a child's mind and life. It allows them to grow with multiple perspectives and layers of knowledge. When you are held accountable for your actions, many times, we try to do better, because better is required by the ones who see better in us!

"Look at a man the way he is, and he only becomes worse,
but look at him as if he were what he could be,
then he becomes what he should be."
~Johann Wolfgang von Goethe"

It's a blessing to have people in our lives, especially the ones who love us unconditionally! Sometimes our strength comes from others believing in us before we can ever believe in ourselves. Sometimes the ability to love, forgive, and sacrifice comes from people loving, forgiving, and sacrificing for us!

"For God so love the world, that He gave His only begotten Son,
that whoever believes in Him should not
perish, but have eternal life."
John 3:16

CHAPTER 12

Deceptive Love

Shortly after I left for college, I met a man who changed my life forever. It was my first serious relationship; my first sexual relationship. It was all consuming, and I didn't realize until too late that it was even consuming ME.

I'm Debbie, and this is my chapter. I'd say it was my story, but my story isn't over. I won the race in my own shoes!

I am writing my own story. I was brought up the middle child in a suburban middle-class family where family, education, and kindness were valued. My parents are still married after fifty-six years. By all accounts, I have always considered myself "average." I was always told that I was smart, and I could do anything I wanted in life, and I believed it. I realize now that I was also very naïve.

I lost myself in a relationship that was so all-encompassing that I didn't realize I was being groomed by a narcissist. I thought I was deeply in love. He was my first. He loved me so much he wanted to be with me all the time! Who could have asked for more? When I heard lines like "I love you so much, let's spend all our time alone together," I fell harder. Slowly, I was distanced from my own family, along with my friends.

I was an excellent musician, in both band and orchestra. That was where I had friends and enjoyed spending time. As the relationship progressed, his jealousy began surfacing. At first, comments such as, "I don't like that you sit next to *Jim*. I'm sure he flirts with you" and "Guys look at you when you dress like that" seemed like simple jealousy—it was kind of sweet. Gradually, these comments became more demanding. He began challenging my choice of clothing and not allowing me to talk to friends. Once, I had a bladder infection, and he was insistent that it was because I had sex with someone else. This type of accusation became very common and was never the truth. I was faithful to him until the end. He would put me down for wanting to raise a family in much the same way I grew up. He'd tease, saying "There's no way we're having three kids and a white picket fence." His mother would make fun of my white cuffed socks, implying I was an uppity suburbanite.

In the music department, we had an honor system message center. This was in 1988, before texting and cell phones. We would leave slips of paper on the wall for other music students. Eventually, I determined that messages left for me were intercepted by him. He would secretly come by while I was in class and take my messages! I'd find out later that someone had messaged me, and to them, it seemed I wasn't interested in whatever the event or message was. Eventually, my friends gave up on me because I never responded. There were other times when my roommate would leave my mail on my desk, and I would find that the envelope steamed open and re-glued shut. He had read my letters, but fighting with him about these things only led to greater damage. The constant accusations of cheating became something I almost believed. He was so convincing!

If I told him I wanted to breakup, he would threaten to drive into a tree, swerving the car so to scare me. I became terrified of what he would do. I attempted to break up multiple times, but he always promised to try harder and would say that he believed me. He always cleaned up for these reconciliations, freshly shaven with jeans and a tucked shirt, which was definitely not the norm. This cycle went on throughout college until eventually I graduated (he didn't). By then, we had been engaged for three years. My one holdout was that I wanted my OWN name on my diploma, so I graduated in April, and we were married in November. He insisted that there be no religion at the wedding, so imagine my horror when our Justice of the Peace came down with laryngitis. She called another judge, who happily filled in but planned on reading The Lord's Prayer during the ceremony. As I walked down the aisle, I remember thinking "If this doesn't work out, I can always get divorced." Foreshadowing much? The judge read The Lord's Prayer, and I was officially a bride in trouble with her groom.

The first few months of marriage were blissful, but the cycle soon repeated. Now that we were married, there were more expectations. I promised never to go on business travel due to his protests. I was accused again and again of cheating. He became more and more violent. We lived in an apartment with holes in the walls and broken dreams. He purposefully left the phone off the hook at night, making me miss the birth of my first nephew. He held me down and did what he wanted with me in the bedroom. I was ashamed and didn't have anyone in which to confide.

The following year as I was climbing the corporate ladder, I was asked to go with a group to Chicago for two weeks to open a new store. I decided that no matter what, I was going to go. I waited until the day before leaving to tell him, and I'm sure he sensed something different in me. He was angry but didn't act out. He even drove me to the place we were meeting and gave me a very demonstrative goodbye. I knew in my heart that would be the last time I would be with him. I called my parents when I got to Chicago and told them what I had done. We made plans for my return.

My parents were, and continue to be, my biggest fans. Leaving an abusive relationship is the most dangerous time for a woman. I shared a little bit of the behind-the-scenes stuff with my parents, but I think they knew all along. The day I moved out, they stood by my side, my dad with baseball bat in hand, and helped me swiftly get what I couldn't live without. We were in and out of that apartment within fifteen minutes. My dad kept watch for the first few nights at my childhood home, making sure we didn't have any surprise guests. It was finally over. Today, I am happily married with three (adult) kids. Sadly, our yard is not fenced, but I do live in my hometown and wear whatever the hell kind of socks I like! I am an elementary special education teacher now, hoping to make a difference in the lives of children.

My dad would always tell me I could do anything I wanted in life. Both my parents made sure I was loved unconditionally.

This gave me the strength to be able to leave, knowing I would have a safe place to land. I have a lot of work to do even though it has been thirty years. I only entered therapy a year ago, and in the thirty years between, I have suffered from low self-esteem and depression. I have developed C-PTSD and work diligently with my therapist to combat these issues. My kids, too, are loved unconditionally. I want them to know they will always have a place to land and that we will always support them in whatever they do. I am a survivor.

Dear Mom & Pops,

I don't know if I ever truly thanked you for the unconditional love and support you gave me thirty years ago. I will never forget how you protected me when I went to move my belongings out of that apartment. Checking behind doors and physically standing guard made me feel confident when all my confidence had been stripped away. There are many, many other examples, but it has been so long, and I have tried my best to bury any memories of that time in my life. I have never shared all the horrible details of it with you, but please know that without you, I would not have been able to live the life I have over these thirty years. I love you to the moon and back, a thousand times. You gave me life—twice.

Dear Mike, Julia, Jessica, and Michael,

Thank you for loving broken me for the past twenty-six (25, 23 & 21) years. I know you have been annoyed, inspired, and sometimes baffled by some of my reactions and thoughts over the years. Perhaps reading this now explains some of that. Regardless, I appreciate you and am incredibly proud of our family. It hasn't always been easy, but we are stronger because of it. Love you all.

Dear Debbie,

You are so strong! Please don't blame yourself for the experiences you had in your earlier life. You didn't know what happening was because narcissists and abusers are incredibly good at what they do. You should be proud of the hard work you are putting into becoming your best self. I know it isn't always easy; but look how far you've come already! Thank you for being patient with yourself and never giving up (even though I know you wanted to a few times). Your kids are amazing adults and your influence on them is priceless. Thank you for finding someone to help you heal your wounds. You are brave, and your story will help others recognize psychological abuse when it is happening to them. I am proud of you.

Love, Me

Author's Notes,

> *"When someone shows you who they are,*
> *believe them the first time."*
> *-Maya Angelou*

Deception will sometimes hide itself right in front of your eyes! It will sometimes wait in the shadows for years before it truly reveals himself. However, when it does tell you it's true identity, and it's not the one you desire, run, and don't stop!

"To take back your power in any given situation,
focus on the things you can control.
The thoughts you choose to think is usually the best place to start"
~Anthon St. Maarten

No matter how bad a situation that we are going through in life, there can always be something that we can hold on to that gives us hope. The possibility that there is a better day coming, the faith, that this too shall pass. We can rely on the love of our God, to know that He will never give us more than we can handle.

The trials and the tribulations that we go through in life, I truly believe, are designed for us and us alone. Everyone has their own cross to carry in life, we can either allow it to drag us down and stay there, or we can start strengthening our mind, body, faith, hope, and confidence. I can only imagine that this is God's way of qualifying us for a greater promise He has in store for us.

"You don't have to fear defeat if you believe it may reveal
powers that you didn't know you possessed."
~Hill Quotes

God's image is imprinted in us all, His strength, His love, His power is with all of us. However, no matter what we go through in life, if we don't summon His presence to spark within us, it will lay dormant, even in our darkest times.

> *"Ask and it will be given to you; seek and you will find; knock and the door will be opened to you."*
> *~Bible, Matthew 7:7 NIV*

CHAPTER 13

The Fall to Purpose

"You'll never impress anyone by doing what they can do," my father said to me, and in my existence, I've discovered no truer words.

"Hold to your vision, and you will make it a reality" and "If something is worth doing, it's worth doing right," my mother said to me, and they are words I live by.

I'm sure you have goals that you're working toward, hopes that will involve elements beyond your control and dreams of what might someday be. It's human nature to strive to be more than we are and achieve a sense of self in which we can feel validation, worth, and fulfillment.

In October of 2012, at the age of twenty-eight, I achieved a goal. I was accepted into the United States Army's Officer Candidate Program after a year of competing with applicants from across the country to attain one of the 250 coveted slots. It had been a nerve-wracking process, from the written exams to the physical tests to a Battalion Board interview with a panel of senior officers and then the final selections. It was the culmination of what felt like a lifetime of work and intention.

I was blessed in my childhood, in that my hippy parents chose to raise my brothers and me with not only a strong ethical and moral compass, but saw fit to teach us the value of life outside of our borders. In multiple year-long adventures in which I was home-schooled, my family traveled tens of thousands of miles. From 1990 through 1992, we sailed roundtrip from Massachusetts to Venezuela, island-hopping along the way. In 1999, we drove a small RV from Gloucester, MA across the USA, down through Mexico, and into the mountains of Quetzaltenango, Guatemala. There, we built a cinderblock house in cooperation with an impoverished family with Habitat for Humanity, and upon our return north, we shoved off on a sailboat for another year of living on the ocean.

Along the way, we had our fair share of life-threatening experiences. When I was six, I was almost eaten by a blacktip shark, but my father and a Scotsman who had joined our crew used pole spears to fight it off. When we were near the coast of Guadeloupe an artillery battery used us for target practice, but I'm pretty sure they were just trying to have some fun at our expense. When we were about fifty miles offshore from Georgetown, Bahamas, pirates attempted to board our boat. However, my father was able to maneuver away under motor as they tried to jump across vessels, and his brandishing of a 12-gauge pump shotgun convinced the men a second pass wasn't in their best interest. In Mexico, we were torn from our RV by Mexican Special Forces soldiers and held at gunpoint as they searched our vehicle for contraband which would label us as Zapatista rebel sympathizers. That checkpoint had been attacked the day before, so we might have disappeared in a ditch if they'd found the Sub-Comandante Marcos dolls I'd bought from an old woman and which my father had hidden under a water tank. However, as my father likes to tell the story, he was with the soldiers inside the RV and just as one of them was reaching into the space where he'd hidden the dolls, another soldier on the roof cried out. The soldier had found a locked box which he clearly suspected contained contraband. Everyone poured outside, and after discovering we only had fireworks and tarps in the container, they sent us on our way.

In my early twenties, I fell in love with wilderness survival and attended over a dozen week-long courses at the Tracker Survival School with a focus on tracking, counter-tracking, and escape and evasion. I then branched out to other schools which taught urban E&E, along with skillsets in lockpicking and getting out of restraint devices. During this time, I became friends with a federal agent who took me under his wing and whose recommendation ultimately tipped the scales in my selection for a ten-week unpaid internship with the Diplomatic Security Service at their headquarters. After college, I tried out for a Special Agent opening, but lacking the managerial life experience of my competitors, I didn't make it past the interview phase. Hence, I pursued an officer position with the United States Army.

When I received the congratulatory phone call from a colonel who told me that I'd made the cut, it was one of the most exciting moments of my life. The weight I'd been feeling for years as I studied and trained without a defined path to a career finally seemed to have lifted.

A few days later, I went longboard skateboarding with a friend, and I had an accident. Almost coinciding with the impact of my face on the pavement was the thought "You idiot! What have you done?" I had detached my jaw on both sides; it was only being held to my face by the skin. My nose was broken, my eye socket was cracked, and four teeth were shattered. Life as I knew it had just ended.

It was a long and agonizing physical recovery, but worse yet, my spirit was broken. I had lost the officer contract and again found myself without purpose or love for life. Having little else, I took a job with a delivery company driving forty-foot box trucks the length of the east coast. It turned out to be everything I despise in a company: a total lack of integrity with a command structure that exploited its weakest members. I quit after a few months, not because I'd found inspiration, but because my values were the only thing I had left, and I couldn't sacrifice my character in trade for a paycheck.

Trying to harness a desire for life again, I focused my energy on finding a way into another passion I've always had. Movies. I started as an extra on an HBO miniseries shot in Massachusetts, and from the perspective of being viewed as a disposable person, I saw and wanted the access that production assistants had on sets. So, I became a production assistant. My first gig was in the Art Department on a feature film where I only got the job because I could drive a box truck. However, I proved myself reliable and utilized my connections to get onto more productions in the commercial world, basically apprenticing under Set Dressers. After a year and a half, I moved into being a PA in the Production Department and a year later, I was hired as a Production Coordinator at a company in New Hampshire.

I never could have maintained this life course if it wasn't for the support of my family, particularly my dad and mom. The life of a PA is hard; the hours are long, and jobs come sporadically, sometimes with weeks at a time out of work. This makes it difficult to do things like have an apartment and keep up with the rent. I was always on call in case an opening came up, and I knew turning an offer down could mean not being selected for a future production... so outside of gig work, a second stable job wasn't feasible.

Having moved back into my parents' house and not needing to worry about rent allowed me to push forward. However, those were the darkest years of my life, and suicide was never far from my mind. It's hard to feel like a man when you're broke, in your young thirties and living at your parents' house while working a job where there is no clear path to advancement and where being powerless and disrespected at your place of employment is par for the course.

I started jumping out of airplanes to just feel alive again. I got licensed in skydiving, and for two years, any money I had post paying bills went to renting parachutes and jump expenses.

In the skydiving world, if you have fewer than 100 jumps, you're considered a novice. There's a lot to learn in every regard, from the gear to the jump to maneuvering in freefall and under canopy. To say skydiving is just falling from the sky is akin to saying Major League Baseball is just two guys playing catch, one guy trying to screw it up and everyone else standing around watching to see how it turns out. Both statements are accurate in the basic sense, but each is also vastly more complex.

I have jumped out of airplanes and helicopters, I've done night jumps and jumps from high altitude where we needed oxygen delivered via nasal cannula tubes on the way up to 22,300 feet... and yet, in my 122 jumps, I have never impressed any of my skydiving friends. Many of my skydiving buddies have between 500 and 10,000 jumps, and I have never done something on a dive that they couldn't also have done. However, in keeping with the notion that "You'll never impress anyone by doing what they can do," the inverse of that statement is to impress them by being good at something they can't do. Hence, a lot of skydiver friends find it pretty cool that I've worked on film sets. In the film industry, I never impressed any of my friends by being a PA or a Coordinator, but they did think it was awesome that I frequently jumped out of airplanes.

In holding true to my vision, in the toughest of times, I think back to why I wanted to be a Special Agent or an Army officer, and I come back to the core aspects of being a good leader: to treat my people well, to do some good in the world while standing up to injustice... and to feel fulfilment in accomplishing something great while harnessing my passions and skillsets. To that end, three years ago, I took a leap of faith, and I left my position as a Production Coordinator. Then I spent nearly every dollar and waking hour in pursuit of becoming the director and producer I wish to be.

I founded a production company, and while taking on little gigs to pay the bills, I dedicated the bulk of my time to producing and directing a documentary. Not having money to pay my crew, I signed the core personnel onto the production with shares in percentages of the potential profit if we can sell the film. I undertook the process of learning to edit and have spent thousands of hours studying, doing, making mistakes, and being better for them. I became an FAA licensed drone pilot and learned cameras so that I wouldn't have to pay an additional professional drone operator a thousand dollars a day during the production. I learned to overcome the hurdles of producing as I devoted thousands of hours to working through issues with insurances, usage rights, contracts, and funding.

There are bright spots in these undertakings. For example, in 2018, capturing a week of live sporting events was going to make or break my documentary, and I had serious concerns about my ability and my local crew's capability to tackle the workload. However, my parents turned their home into a bed and breakfast/production office, and my mentors Francine Loretero (a fantastic director and producer) and her husband Bill Schreck (an excellent cinematographer), flew cross country to stay with us for the week. In addition, their friend and mentor Billy Graham sponsored me nearly fifty thousand dollars' worth of production gear, cameras, and drones, and sent two drone pilots along with the equipment to help out. If not for their generosity, I have no doubt that my production would have suffered, and I would have missed out on the valuable learning experience of directing a dozen person crew. It was one of the most empowering moments of my existence, and now, after personally dedicating more than 6,000 hours to this project, I estimate that I'm only about 500 hours away from the end of post-production on a feature length documentary. It has been the hardest thing I have ever undertaken in my life, but as my mom says, "If something is worth doing, it's worth doing right."

In the future, I look forward to harnessing my skillsets in order to tackle projects in which I can do some good, help some people, treat my crew well, and bring the audience along for the experience.

To my father and mother, I'd like to say thank you. You've been there for me in my darkest hours, months, and years. We didn't always get along or see eye to eye, but I know I wouldn't still be here without you. I value how you taught me a system of knowing right from wrong in which practicing empathy and viewing situations from multiple angles factored into discovering the best truth of a matter. Our vast travels imprinted on my young mind the scale of cultures in existence beyond our own and put in perspective the hardships we faced versus the enormity of issues people of third world nations contend with on a daily basis. You tempered my hot-headed idealist nature with practical concerns and convinced me time and again that I can do more to help people in this world with a camera in my hands instead of a weapon. So, as you get older and make peace with your eventual passing from this life, know that through my actions and the people I will help and protect, your influence lives on.

Sean O.

Author's Notes,

"It's not our abilities but persistence that ultimately
leads us to our greatest achievements."
~Apoorve Dubey"

In life, we'll face many failures that beat us to the ground, the majority of people will stop, but there are only a select few who will pick themselves up, dust themselves off, and find the strength to climb the next mountain in hopes to get to the top.

"It ain't about how hard you hit: It's about how hard
you can get hit and keep moving forward. It's how
much you can take and keep moving forward.
That's how winning is done."
~Rocky Balboa, Sylvester Stallone, Rocky

It's one of the hardest hits we take in life when we set high goals for ourselves and don't achieve them. It's easy in that moment to blame life, God, and your current circumstances, but when you have people who care about you, love you, they will be the ones who will be your rock to help you get back up every time you fall.

Sometimes, the things that we think we want and strive for in life but don't achieve we see as failure. The question is, do you believe that to be true or false? I truly believe that the things that we don't get weren't meant for us to have, because they would have stopped us from discovering the things we were born to do.

"Five questions every human being must answer—
who am I, where am I from, why am I here,
what can I do, where am I going?"
~Dr. Myles Munroe

Many times, we strive for things that we see others do, the things that look cool and popular. We try to fit in with the crowd of the cool kids, we try to be a member of a certain club that we know deep in our heart is not for us. So why? Why do it, instead of doing the things that we know is in us and that we are good at?

I've experienced in my own life that standing out is a lonely journey to take. Being who you are and the person you were created to be is a challenge, especially when no one else understands you. So why be different? It took years to learn, believe, and accept that God never intended for us to be the same! God puts everyone on this earth with their own unique gifts and qualities. We all have a place, and we all have our part to play. If we were all the same, we wouldn't evolve, we wouldn't explore, we wouldn't dare to attempt the impossible!

"It's always seems impossible until it's done."
~Nelson Mandela

So this is the truth, we're all made special in HIS image, and HE is everything—the now, the forever, the Creator, the Possible, the "I AM."

CHAPTER 14

Caged Bird

It was our first Christmas as Mr. and Mrs. I was so excited to see what the man I decided to settle down with got me. It came in a not so big box, so I just knew it was something fancy. When I ripped off the paper, the box read Fog Light Bulbs. I chuckled because I thought he had my sense of humor and used the box as a clever way to disguise something greater. Boy was I wrong, I did, in fact, receive a set of fog lights for my vehicle that first Christmas. That was the only gift I received. At that moment, I knew nothing great was coming from this.

Hello, my name is Kat W. Tweety, Cherry for short. This is my story. My story of how I grew into my shoes.

Like most eighteen-year-olds, I graduated from high school ready to take over the world. I had goals, I had aspirations, but not one of those have I yet achieved. My life was put on hold. I learned quickly that life is like a jar of jalapenos, what you eat today could very well burn your ass tomorrow. I have a motto to never live life with regrets but with lessons learned.

This lesson started twenty-one years ago when I made the choice to marry, not for love; but for convenience. Dropping out of college to pursue a modeling career, then becoming a single mom after a sexual assault, only to become pregnant again by who was supposed to stay a smash buddy, I believed I had no other options. On my wedding day, people were buzzing around, excited, dressed in their beautiful African attire of purple and gold. The large Church was packed, and I had not one friend in the building. It was mainly family and my parents' friends. A small bit of his family was in attendance, only because the best man drove two hours to pick them up. My parents bought his mom a dress and the nephew some shoes, his sister refused to wear her head wrap because she just got her hair done the day before. I was six months pregnant when I walked down the aisle in my beautiful mermaid style gown with the princess train. The only thoughts I had in my head as both my parents held my hand down the red velvet aisle were—I won't be married long, I'm not going to stay, divorce is always an option. The rest of the day was a blur. I vaguely remember us cutting the cake and my parents dancing to the song "Hit the road, Jack."

As the years went by, four more children passed through my vaginal canal. We decided it would be best for me to stay at home and raise the five children due to the cost of daycare. That almost became my death sentence. His mother had told him that those were my children and that he need not worry about them but to take care of himself, get his education, and do what he needs to do. So, he did just that. Because of his job, we moved around a lot. So, I didn't make many friends. My main interaction was with the kids and some of the other adults when I volunteered at the school.

The days began running together, everyday seemed like a groundhog's day. I ran the house like a well oil machine. We wake up, I cook breakfast we do daily devotion before we go off to school, then the ones who were left home watched TV or play while I clean house, then I make lunch and we have nap, then wake up to pick up from school, fix dinner, eat by 5:00, clean up, get ready for bed, then sleep again. Every day the same thing with some added kids' activities at times while he went to work and focused on his education. He had no worries at home because I had everything taken care of. With all of that, he showed no appreciation, no thank yous, no I appreciate you, no good job, no public accolades at award banquets in his honor. His co-workers received more recognition than I did. I would sit at the banquet and watch him hand out flowers and gift to the people who worked around him while I got nothing.

Obviously, we had sex because children came from it, but for me, sex was more like a chore. I slowly began to lose myself, my self-worth, my dignity my self-love. I used to think that was probably my fault, I should have played the helpless damsel and not be so strong. For years, I built this man up from nothing to something great. People around the world read his name in magazines, but my name is nowhere written. I had put my life on hold. My life was on hold to make sure I raised my children up to love and respect God. My life was on hold as I built this man up from an associate's degree to a PhD.

Holidays and my birthday I stopped looking forward to. When you receive gifts like Lay's potato chips, Oreos and peanut M&Ms for these so-called special occasions, you start to not look forward to them. I couldn't stand to see others happy on social media. It took so much for me to wake up each day and start my routine.

The first time I attempted to take my life, the Lord gave me a glimpse of what my children's life would be like if I left them, and it horrified me. I felt like a beautiful vibrant colored macaw parrot that was housed inside of a small elaborate designed antique cage. No room to spread any wings or grow. I just existed, I wasn't living.

I knew I had sunk to the bottom when I started to plan his death. For weeks, I would drive through this one particular intersection at different times of the day and study the lights and the traffic patterns. My plan was to have him in the passenger seat and run the red light. I wanted him dead, but just me injured. I knew then I needed to seek professional help. I got on antidepressant medication, and that helped for a little bit because I was self-medicating, not taking it on a daily. I kept looking for the next high to keep me going. I didn't turn to drugs, but I turned to caffeine and I binged on peanut M&Ms for nine months. All I ate, breakfast lunch and dinner, and everything in between, was that yellow bag of peanut M&M's. I was at the point of eating the ten pound party pack in one day and be looking for another for the next day.

It was a cold winter that year, and I had ran out of my stash, and the roads were too bad to make it to any late-night convenience store, so for a couple of days I had to go without. I ended up passing out from the caffeine withdrawal. The lining of my stomach was almost eaten away completely. The ulcers in my stomach were the size of fifty cent pieces. The H pylori stomach infection that I had twice almost did me in. After that long road of recovery, I was still in that cage, and I was still looking for a way out and some happiness.

I had been speaking to God on a regular, and he had been answering my prayers, but I just wasn't satisfied because I still was in that house. I then began looking for happiness in other people. I know the Lord doe not condone adultery, but he does place people in your life for a reason and a season. Jedi is the man I had wanted to marry several years ago. Our paths had crossed a couple of times. On this particular third time our path crossed, we began to build a relationship. He was married with children, I was married with children, but neither one of us wanted to be there. For seven years, we leaned on each other and continued our affair. Jedi allowed me to see that I was stronger than I thought. He motivated me, he encouraged me, he filled those voids that the other didn't. Jedi bent the antique bars of that birdcage for me so I could stretch my wings just enough to remember that I can fly.

I recall the straw that broke the camel's back. All seven of us drove down to Florida to spend Christmas with my family and celebrate our fifteenth wedding anniversary. I chose not to purchase the children's gifts until after we got down there because it would be easier for me. He never liked me spending his money, but what choice did I have, because I didn't have a job. For five children and him, I spent $875 total on everyone's gifts. It's not like we didn't have it, like I said; he just didn't want me spending it. So, to punish me like he did so many other times, for this anniversary, his original thought was not to get me anything at all. After my dad had a come to Jesus meeting with him, he decided to go to the store, Walgreens to be exact. He walked through the front door with gift bag in hand and asked me to come back to the bedroom, he had something for me. I had already given him my gift for the anniversary, a nice gold watch. I should have known better from previous anniversaries. I follow him back to the bedroom, and he places the gift on the bed, smiled, and said "happy anniversary." It was a beautiful bag with beautiful pink, purple, white, and green tissue paper fluffed up so neatly out of the bag. The card read some sentimental factory processed thought that I knew he didn't mean. I began to pull the tissue paper out one by one, and when I reach the bottom where the gift was. I pulled out a can of planters peanuts. If Chester, my gun, was on my hip that day, he would have been blown away, blood splattered all over my mom and dad's beautiful yellow walls. I was too angry to say anything, so I just walked out. That day, I prayed harder than I had ever prayed before.

I began praying to the Lord for strength, for wisdom, for boldness to make moves to get out of the unhealthy situation. In the next six years, I made it a point to lean solely on God to build me up. I began making moves in silence like lasagna, not letting the right hand know what the left hand is doing. The more I praised the Lord and the more he blessed me, the more I cried out to him, the stronger he made me.

Two years later, we separated, because his job took him to the other side of the country, and I chose to stay behind and then move back down to Florida to continue raising my children. Fear, I did not have, because the Lord began to open and shut doors that I never had access to before. For so long, this man had been living on an island in the middle of his family. We were just there. I knew he really didn't care about us when we attended his retirement party and the head of his organization came to me and asked me who I was. When I told him I am the wife and these are the three of the five children, he was floored. "He never said he had a family," said the gentleman. I wasn't angry when I heard that, I was relieved. It just made what I was about to do much easier.

Without any help from him, I was tasked to prepare and sell our home. This was something completely new to me, but I did not worry because the Lord placed in my path a realtor who took care of everything and made the process so smooth. The kids and I packed up and made that sixteen-hour journey South to relocate to Florida. Throughout that whole transition, I asked the Lord what to do, how to do it, and when to do it, and He showed me every step of the way. This relocation was going to be the make or break, and I had refused to break. I needed to see if this little bird was strong enough to make it outside of that cage. For two years, the kids and I lived in peace and happiness. I was free, I thought, I was making it on my own with just his money. After his retirement, he decided to move back in, and I refused to go back into my cage after I'd been out briefly. On January 3rd 2019, the Lord gave me strength to walk into a lawyer's office and file for divorce. He was served with papers a few weeks later. He was extremely angry. I thought he would get the hint and move out or at least sleep on the in another room, that would have been too much like right. That night, I slept, or tried to, on one side of the bed as he refused to let me close my eyes until I had sex with him. Yes, he forced himself on me. The next morning, I gathered some of my clothes and moved into the game room, and that's where I slept on the couch for three months. I was so ashamed to have my children see me sleeping on the couch where they once sat playing video games. My son expressed his disgust and anger seeing his mom curled up with blankets draped on her, but it made no difference to his dad. By the grace of God, I was able to purchase a sofa sleeper which made for much better sleep.

Even though he and I didn't speak, tensions remained high in the house, the kids felt it every time they walked in the house. It got to the point where I couldn't keep subjecting myself and my kids to this torment. I took him to court for temporary assistance so I could move out. Thank you, Jesus, I found a house in my budget just a mile away, so no one had to change schools.

During the year and half of the divorce process, I dated and slowly began to get my groove back. I finally felt like I had some self-worth. I grew even closer to Jesus, I grew stronger, became bolder, wiser, and learned so much about me, myself, and I. When I got to the point of true self-love that is when the Lord said to me "It is time." Enter stage right, Mr. Old Navy, we met on a dating sight. I quickly noticed this man was nothing like the man I was detaching myself from. He is God fearing and appreciates me. We became friends before lovers. We talk, we laugh, we cry, motivate, and support each other. I know now what it means to be in Love. If I get the opportunity to walk down that red velvet aisle again, this time it will be because of love.

My life has completely turned around. This bird had finally gotten out of the cage. Her wings had grown in, and she has been flying so high and hard that she knocked over and broke that damn cage. NO more will I allow someone to rob me of my joy or take me to a point of complete darkness. The Lord had carried me through these twenty-one years, where he taught me to be a stronger woman of faith. I now know that I can do all things through Christ who strengthens me.

October 14, 2020 I finally grew into my shoes, and this chapter is done.

Thank you again for this opportunity! I pray it's a blessing to someone because it was a blessing for me to share it.

Sincerely,

Kat W. Tweety

Author's notes,

> "How you treat someone in a relationship is usually the
> way you want to be treated, or deserve to be treated."
> ~DMA"

It's been said time and time again, "treat others how you'd like to be treated." Some people hear it, know it, but tend to forget it when it really matters.

Committing to someone, and giving them your all in the name of love is an amazing thing, if they truly deserve it. Many of us have made mistakes in relationships because what we thought was love turned out to be a game of give me, give me, and no return.

At a certain point, we must all know our value and have an identity of who we are and what we know we deserve in life. It's only then that we can start to set standards for ourselves and truly put the maximum value on our lives. Our value is not something that can be bought, we are not defined by a dollar sign, we are priceless! It must be earned, and only then will it be a gift that's given to that one special person who has proven themselves worthy of receiving it!

God made all of us special in our own way! My special is different from yours, and yours different from the next person. It's the reason why even if you're an identical twin, your finger prints are still different!

Finding out who you are and knowing how special you are will forever be one of the greatest discoveries in this world, not just for you, but for so many others! This person that you are, have become, or are seeking to find has within unlimited power to make a difference in this world. We're all bred from royal lineage, because we've all been created by our King, God almighty, who is, and always will be!

No-one should ever be given the power to treat us any different, unless we allow it! This new you will know and believe I am special, I am beautiful, I am confident, successful, happy, healthy, and I am a child of the Most High!

CHAPTER 15

143 Conquering Love

My name is Pat, and this is my story.

I won my race in the shoes of one of my closest friends; Michael "Duk" Tran.

I am a self-driven, highly motivated, creative individual who is a go-getter in life from the time the sun goes up to the time the sun goes down. Mike was full of laughter, happiness, love, and care for everything and everyone around him. No matter what he had going on in his life; he made not only time for his best friends and family but, strangers of all types.

My Junior year of college, I was madly in love with who I thought was the love of my life at the time. As time went on... I started to change the path of my own treasure map. I say this in a matter of changing my dreams and goals so someone else could have theirs. As time went on in our relationship, things got super serious. I found us drifting apart from one another fast. I started to beat myself up mentally, emotionally, and physically, because I felt blinded by all of these false perceptions of "the love of my life" I once thought were positive.

The relationship ended up spiraling out of control, until one day I woke up to her telling me she wasn't happy anymore. That it wasn't me she wanted to be with for the rest of her life. All I could think about was how much I sacrificed to be with her. At this point in time, we had a house together and two cats. While I was in midst of planning the next ten years to be with her, I found out she was planning on the next ten days to be away.

As we got closer and closer to our wedding, because we agreed we were going to work things out, she ends up not coming home one night. Three days later, I find out that she has been seeing another man. At this point in time, we are less than a couple months from our wedding, and everything I sacrificed to be with her was so far out of the picture. I knew it was going to be impossible to get my life back.

One morning, I decided I was done living with her, and I packed one bag of clothes in a backpack. I decided I was going to leave my entire life behind me. Unfortunately, little did I know—I left my soul behind as well.

I've been in the hospitality Industry my entire life. As soon as I was legal to work; I got a job as a dishwasher. For anyone who doesn't know or understand the life in the restaurant industry... It is full of long nights that are followed up with drugs, sex, and alcohol. This industry also meant everything to me; as I treated it as an escape from all of the stress, sadness, and disappointment in my life. It allowed me to be whoever I wanted to be.

I had always been known to carry myself different than most. Didn't get in the drinking scene until college, didn't smoke until I was in my twenties, and I did my best to stay away from drugs. All of that changed once I left/felt like I had lost my soul. I felt that I was giving up on myself and God. I felt worthless. My friends were picking me up on the side of the street on a weekly basis because I was "blacking out" from drinking almost overnight. The majority of my friends sold recreational drugs for a living. So I knew I had access to anything I wanted. I made myself believe that I wasn't addicted, that I didn't have a problem, that I could control it all. In reality, I did have a problem. I just learned how to be someone I wasn't. I just wanted people to like me and have fun with me… so, I made that my priority in life. I threw away all my dreams, and there was still no sight of them ever coming back. Unfortunately for me, I became one of the best functioning alcoholic junky, one would say.

Then one day, a gentleman walked into the restaurant I worked at the time. I was the company head trainer for FOH operations, so I had the opportunity to meet every applicant and every new hire for the organization. This gentlemen had that feel, the vibes, the energy that less than 1% have.

My entire life, my family had always lectured me on the people I surrounded myself with; that they weren't good for me and they wouldn't take me anywhere in life that I should be going toward. What my family didn't know and didn't see was the good in people and the WHO about someone. It's not about what you do in my opinion; it's about who you are. Where I'm from, unfortunately, people get those two mixed up all the time.

Every year at the restaurant up to the day this gentleman walked in the door... I led in almost every category in sales. I was obsessed with work and perfecting every part of what I knew. In reality, I was replacing my sadness with work and money that I would spend on drugs and alcohol. Little did I know... There was someone out there who was even more obsessed. That gentleman's name was Michael "Duk" Tran; my best friend. The one who taught me what life should be about.

As I was prioritizing my down time after work to getting drunk and hanging out with friends until six in the morning and then waking up at nine to work a double the next day... I found I now had a new friend to join me in the madness way to live. The only difference was... He didn't drink. NOT AT ALL. But, he was always out and about. He was always there for everyone and anyone. He worked his crazy eighty-hour weeks and then partied with us every single night.

As time went on, we found that we were building a great friendship of trust, happiness, and energy. He taught me how to live and love life again. He taught me how time was only a number and how anything can be achievable. He taught me how all it takes is "one more step" to get to the next level.

I found myself going to bars less, doing less drugs, exercising more, and getting back into my passion of life, which is cooking. I even ended up going back to the same school I had originally left for my ex-fiancée to finish up and be able to say I didn't give up. Mike showed me how to be hungry again. How never to settle for anything and to love everyone who comes into your circle.

One day, I woke up with a phone call. It was a dark rainy day… The General Manager of the restaurant I worked at the time had called my cell phone directly. As he is crying…. he goes on and tell me that Mike just passed away at age thirty-one. In absolute disbelief, I refused to believe it. All I could think about was why and how?

Mike's health had been declining fast. He ended up having a pill addiction. Most of my friends had pill addictions at the time. It was common in the restaurant industry with opioids. Unfortunately for Mike… his addiction was on the next level as he passed away on an "H-Bomb"(heroin and extasy combo). The police found him dead in his apartment after he called 911 while trying to iron his apron so he could get to work.

While Mike had changed my life through several heart to hearts and amazing memories… he had been facing a battle for years and years himself. He always told me "one step at a time." That is how life should be lived.

Once he passed, I was given the honor to cremate his body. As Buddhist monks and his family prayed for his soul… That day, I promised myself I was going to stop living other peoples' dreams. That I was going to get my life back and find life in my soul once again.

Here we are several years later… There is not one second of the day that I don't think Mike is next to me. Mike was an angel sent by God to help me with my life. I've been not only able to change my own life around, but I've been able to help many others with their drug and alcohol addictions.

Prior to getting engaged and falling into darkness, my dream was to own my own restaurant one day. To be a world-class chef. While that dream seemed lost and unachievable years ago. I now have not only conquered addiction, depression, anxiety, and fear, but I have built a beverage business from the ground up, and I am in the process of starting a non-profit.

Mike's server number or employee number was "143." Later on, I found that there were several meanings behind that number. First of all "143" means "I love you." Also, David 143 in the bible talks about addiction and how to conquer them. Ironic? I don't think so. My non-profit will be called 143.

Three things Mike said to me often were: When life is beating you down and you think you have nothing left... dig deeper. Pain doesn't matter, because it doesn't hurt.

Love everyone, including yourself. One step at a Time

Mike taught me never to give up, no matter what. And to always show up. showing up is the most difficult part; but if you can do that... You are already ahead.

If it wasn't for you stepping into my life... I most likely wouldn't be here. I would be next to you in heaven. Or at least I would have hoped I made it that far. Thank you for giving me the courage to be different. Thank you for rescuing me from the mistakes you made. Thank you for showing me the value in life and how every second of the day means something or has value.

Even though my life spiraled out of control, I was able to find light and purpose because of you. You brought joy in everyone's life every second of the day. You showed up every day, regardless of what was happening in your own life.

I wish you had asked for help. You never said bye to me, and I never said bye to you, because I know you are always right next to me. Thank you for your shoes. I'm going to finish the race for you and impact as many lives as I can, just like you did.

This is why I'm certain you are my angel and always have been. I love you 143.

Author's notes,

"Never allow someone to be your priority while allowing yourself to be their option."
~Mark Twain

Love, is the most powerful substance in this universe, it can make us believe things that we can't see, see things that don't exist, and do things we never thought possible! Love comes in many different forms and strength. We have the ability to generate it within us, and natural receptors to receive it from others! Love has the ability to conquer, cure, and create. This substance has the ability to take any man or woman to the highest levels of their lives in an instant. However, when the high is gone, it can feel as if you're falling from the sky at Mach speed without a parachute!

Our creator is the source of all love, because He is love, and because He made love a part of us, within us. Even though we may have lost what someone else gave us, we don't have to fall, we can learn to grow wings on the way down. All we need to do is go back to the source of all love, and He'll never allow us to fall.

"Death leaves a heartache no one can heal,
love leaves a memory no one can steal."
~ Richard Puz

God has a way of using others to convey His message to us. Many times, we ask for a miracle, and because it isn't what we imagined, we tend not to know when it's being given to us! It's been said that "people come in our lives for a reason and a season."

I've learned the hard way to value the people who are in our lives, because we truly don't know what tomorrow may have in store for them.

When we have people we care about, it's necessary to honor them as much as possible when they're living. A simple thank you, I appreciate you, and most importantly, even though it's hard for most to say, I love you!

This book was written exactly for this purpose! Life is short, and we can't wait for the best or right moment to appreciate someone for who and what they mean to us! I heard this quote once before, but unsure who said it.

"In a week, there is a Monday, Tuesday, Wednesday,
Thursday, Friday, Saturday, and a Sunday,
however there is no Someday, or a Oneday."
~ Unknown Author

Make today the day to share with someone how much they mean to you in your life! Every second counts, make them your priority!
"I LOVE YOU, GOD LOVES YOU!"

CHAPTER 16

Manufactured Happiness

I remember wanting to make sure that everyone was happy with the choices that I made. As a child, I was a tomboy. I wanted nothing to do with frilly dress, Bobby socks, patent leather shoes, princesses, or anything if that nature. I wanted to ride bikes, was okay in the dirt, was okay with football with the neighborhood boys, and have my version of fun.

Yet, my mother wanted me to do ballet, so I did. I didn't care for it. I learned to tolerate it as a way to have her be happy that I chose something she may have liked. Who knew such a decision at such a young age, would continue for decades?

At the age of ten, I experienced the death of someone close to me. Someone I knew in the neighborhood where I lived. I was talking to this person as I walked through the neighborhood. By the time I walked home, which was no more than ten minutes, if that, the Jews shot his body dead in the front yard of the house where we were talking. He wasn't even eighteen years old.

That is when I knew that the safety of my neighborhood was no longer as safe as I thought it was. As I watched, my parents had their discussion about why this could have happened, not knowing that I was in that area at any point. To hear their views with a thought of "If I stayed a little longer, could that have been me" going on at the same time, I realized that I was not going to be the same. It felt like I had to do what made me happy, but also wanted to make my parents happy, too. What a fine line to walk at such a young age.

My name is K. Patterson, and this is my story. I won the race in the shoes of my Paternal grandmother.

My Paternal Grandmother was not a simple woman. She has a gentle side but was very no nonsense. She did not take sides in our family, no one was treated differently. She raised five boys through the 30s and into the 80s. Much was seen in her lifetime. During the years, she and my grandfather were also foster parents. They only wanted boys. The ones no one else wanted or could handle. I have seen her have even the roughest and toughest showing manners and following rules. She was never lenient and knew that she couldn't show weakness. I watched her and realized that this is how I developed into who I am.

She was not "feisty," she spoke her mind and was unapologetic. She was a leader and would make something out of nothing. She was not scared to get her hands dirty and was determined to show her independence.

I know that she was not perfect, but her story is the reason she is the way that she is and why I know a walk in her shoes was no easy task. Losing both parents before the age of eighteen, marrying and having a child before the age of twenty at the end of the Great Depression, then two more children during and after WWII, as her husband fought in that war. All five of her children serving in the military. Some going into wars. Yet, she had her faith to keep her, as well as her survival skills.

My grandmother kept everything to make sure it was remembered. I loved going to her house. I was able to explore and find things, learn, read, ask questions, and be able to enjoy and have fun. The only thing that I could not do was watch "The Stories."

Sitting in their porch with them and seeing those in the neighborhood greet as they walked by or stop to talk to them was amazing to me. I wanted that sense of community where I lived. We knew our neighbors, but it wasn't the same feeling or energy as what I observed at their house. People would stop by just to chat, drop something off, or just to say hello. There was no one age range. They would even have some of the foster boys who they raised stop by and show them love and give them updates.

My grandmother never worked, but she volunteered in various capacities. When she was younger, she owned a bicycle shop in Jackson Ward. She was always wanting to hire someone Black when having something repaired. It was those things that allowed me to know the importance of supporting those who resemble me (not just my upbringing).

My grandmother never judged anyone's situation and was willing to help with all she had, whether it was a hot meal, a place to stay, a phone call, or just the need to talk. Yet, she did not mince words and would say what needed to be said.

As a teenager, I decided that I would hang with those whom I was most comfortable. That happened to be boys. There weren't any particular boys, but in my high school, people had neighborhoods they were From. I decided to be cool with someone from each neighborhood; it actually just naturally happened that way. I wasn't judged. I felt safe, and I felt comfortable. I could be myself and not feel a need to "fit in." I had girls I hung with, as well. Yet, I spent more time with the guys in my classes and at lunch.

This led to some choices that weren't great for a child to make, and as I got older, as young adult who wasn't considering all that she really had to lose, that fine line I was walking to please my parents disappeared. I was doing my own thing. Yet, trying to be somewhat mindful. In this time, I was making some decisions that could have had me in some very toxic or worse predicaments. Yet, my grandmother would always let me know that she was praying for me.

I did not realize it at the time, but the prayers she put into the Universe made the Universe listen and keep me from dire harm. Looking back, there are multiple situations where I could have been seriously hurt or possibly not here to even write this. Writing this now and knowing someone I know will read it makes me nervous.

Once I was privileged to become a mother, I knew I had to be different. Despite all of my shenanigans, I graduated high school and college. It was not an easy journey, and it cost me a lot of money out of my pocket. I was able to understand the sacrifices that needed to be made and that I can't put myself in situations where I may not see another day in the outside or on this earth.

My grandmother was getting older, and her telling me that she wouldn't dare want to bury her grandchild, let alone one of her own children in her lifetime, my gosh, what a statement to make you wake up and try to do better. That made me realize that even without telling anything and making everything look like it's all good, she could see right through it. She observed. She paid attention. She was in tune and intuitive. The thought of wasting years and not being to see her or be around her made me nervous. She held the family together. My grand-mother was the glue. Even if you wanted to hate her, you still respected her.

I am a mother of two. I achieved a post graduate degree. I am able to provide for my children with assistance from my family and my own village/tribe. That sense of making sure you have community support and can support your commu-nity is within me. She instilled that in me. I try to "Buy Black" as much as I possibly can. Telling stories and memories if her allows me to stay connected and realize that I carry on her leg-acy every day. I have her and my other grandparents tatted on my shoulders because I shoulder their legacies every day. My grandmother may not be famous, but she will be remembered.

In her remembrance, I try to see the lesson in all that hap-pens. There is no time to dwell in what is wrong, you have to figure out what can be done, make a way to get what's needed and use your resources. Educate yourself, because school will only teach you so much. Do your own research because relying on the words of man can lead you into a place you never want to be and may be hard to leave from. Support others and know they will remember you when it's needed, even if you don't ask or show need. Be better than the generation before you. You cannot grow and do/be better if you are stuck in what was or what has been. Know who you are and who you want to be. Make sure you leave a mark in this earth when you are gone.

Dear Grandma,

I know that it may not have been said enough but THANK YOU. You have taught me so much about life while on this Earth and even since you have been gone. I know I haven't lived up to all that you may have wanted, yet I know that no matter what; every accomplishment made you proud. You made so much out of nothing or just a little so many times. I learned so much from you that I can't even think of it all. You allowed me to be myself. You allowed me to explore, discover, imagine, and enjoy life. I want the same for my children. I'm able to speak for myself and be un-apologetic about my feelings and thoughts. I miss you so much. Please know that I will never forget you. I'll never forget all that I observed that I take with me and shoulder every single day. Up until your death, you didn't complain. You still lived and were still as much of you as you could possibly be. I wish I had more time with you. Your live was pure, unconditional, and abundant. You didn't have to say it for me or anyone else to see and feel it.

I know I can't fill your shoes, but I'm running this race in the ones you left for me to use. I am forever grateful that you were and are my grandmother.

Love, Khari

Author's notes,

Many times, we try to be something that we aren't because we think it's what will make someone else happy. I've come to realize in life that trying to make someone else happy is a fulltime job and a never-ending task. It will drain you, consume you, take, and use your value time that you have on this earth. The time that you will never get back, the time that no matter what, when it's gone; there is no rewind button to get it back.

"I cannot give you the formula for success, but I can give you the formula for failure – which is: Trying to please everybody." - Herbert Bayard Swope

There is only one person that you can be in this world, and that is you! However, so many times, so many people have not defined who they are and take the identity of someone they truly aren't.

One of the best things that I discovered in my life was to find someone who embody the qualities that I thought were admirable. Qualities that represented something good; honor, courage, values, integrity, and most important—having a love for God.

Not everyone will represent those qualities, sometimes you may have to find them from several people, but when you get around it, you'll automatically know that you found it, because it's attracted to you like a magnet. It's a feeling that's hard to understand until you experience it, but just know that the reason why you are attracted to it is because it has always been in you and a part of you.

We can also learn, from negativity, because sometimes the negative people in our lives, drive us away from becoming negative ourselves. Learn what not to do and know their negative energy that you feel inside. The one where you will do whatever it takes to avoid them is like the opposite side of a magnet that repels away from you.

The ability to do better and be better is simple a choice! Yes, your environment and situations play a role in everything we do and become, but at a certain point, the decision is truly up to you. It takes courage to change, it takes courage to move away from something that you're comfortable with. However, if you decide to take this path, just know it's always going to be better to take it with God by your side. It's not always easier, but once you commit, it's guaranteed!

CHAPTER 17

Relentless Survivor

An Allowed Perspective

The year was 1984, abandoned at age two. Later in life (2018), learning from my birth mother that she made this choice because she could no longer go through bathing my older brother William and I in gas station sinks and feeding us peanut butter and jelly sandwiches while spending winter nights in a car with the heat on. She had one of two other sons on the way, my younger brothers Jermaine and Kenny. The circumstances were taking their toll, and she could not afford the gas to keep the car running the whole night.

Placed in the hospital before going into foster care, I got out of my crib and pulled a heater down on me, and the hot water burned my lower abdomen, needing skin grafts. I went into foster care after this in Prince Georges county Maryland's system. There, I was beaten, sexually abused, and locked in a room and eventually a cage. My brother William and I would spend our days playing with shoes on our hands for toys and eating paper, alone all day. When we would be fed, it was always grits and peas. I had no concept of numbers, colors, or even what a birthday was, let alone my own. My skin was yellow, my teeth rotten, eyes so sensitive I needed to wear sunglasses well into my later childhood years and could not be outside for very long without getting sick. The physical abuse endured was beatings to the point of not being able to sit, the mother taking me into the bathroom and filling up the bathtub with hot water and placing me in it naked, only to urinate in it as I sat in the water. Later in life, I began having nightly nightmares for an entire summer and then as an adult for over three years, though only three times a week. In these dreams, I would always be fighting an unseen woman (I just knew it was a woman), she had her hands around my throat and was sitting on top of me. I fought for my life in these dreams. For many years, a family member of mine believed that I was being attack by a demon and was having mystics in her church send me tapes of prayers to send them (demons) away. It was not until much later in life that I did the work with these, and much more was revealed. The dreams were that of the woman choking me and holding me under water in that bathtub. I had three images of this but went my whole life believing it was a dream and not part of my experience. After deciding to do the work, I realized these did happen and not just three times but near nightly. This foster home was within a Black family. They had an older son (or other foster child), I would put his age at 16-17. He would sexually abuse me, as I also had images of these experiences. These were "closer" in my mind, so I never doubted the experience of them.

Near the age of five, I and my older half-brother William, who is also bi-racial, were adopted into my now family with two White parents. They had three other kids; two older sisters and one older brother. All but my oldest sister was bi-racial. I attached immediately to my mother and my oldest sister. For a period, things were calm, and a space that I had never felt before. My aunt Enid and my uncle Ansley came to our house one time, I must have been six maybe seven at this point. They came to meet William and I. As they were walking up the stairs outside, I saw them through the screen door and ran in fear. Fear that was fear of losing my life. They were Black from Guyana. I hid behind furniture in our history room and cried for my sister, wanting them to stay away from me. I only saw the color of their skin; I had no idea that they were a completely different Black couple. Up to that point in my life, I could not recall the faces of the foster care people, as I did not look up much out of fear. I only recalled legs and arms. Aunt Enid and Uncle Ansley matched them by color. I believed that they were the Black woman and man from the foster care home and that they were coming to take me back. I did not allow myself to be close to them until much later in my childhood.

Things stayed calm for a while in my new home. I began to feel safe and experienced new sites and ways of being, and FUN. I was learning numbers and colors and eating meat. Most of my interactions were with my oldest sister and my mother. They devoted the most time to me. I had not real relationship with my father for multiple reasons. I had no positive male experiences, and he did not show much interest in getting to know me. Later, he admitted that he did not want to adopt William and I, if it had been up to him. This comment matched how I had felt as a kid.

Back to the first period of calm and stability in my life. This time, I was growing in many areas of my life, catching up in school. This lasted for only so long. Shortly after, my older adoptive brother began sexually abusing me in his room, my second oldest sister, who has a mental disability, began beating me mercilessly. One time so bad she slammed my head into a doorknob, and I believe that knocked me out. My older brother William, who I was so close to in foster care and at beginning of our adoption, began to fight and beat me almost every morning. All three would also fight and hit my mother and oldest sister. There the calmness and peace went again. There was no stability.

Looking back, every day I woke up wondering who was going to attack me, who would yell or act out. Both my oldest brother, being bi-polar, and for some reason my second oldest sister would "switch" what felt like hourly from normal to all-out rage. I never knew what to expect. I developed a mindset that my life would be up to me, I had to rely on myself. I was on a swim team during all this and spending much of the summers with my older sister at her pool. At the beginning, we went to Oxon Hill swim club, which was private. It was an all-White club. They asked my mother not to bring us back because we were Black. We then had to join Temple Hills swim club because it was publicly owned. I looked forward to going there and getting away from my home and all the unrest and the lack of communication, from the top down. I enjoyed playing soccer and being a kid. As I got older, the abuse and unrest became less and less. Though there was no real communication. Our house was often quiet. Some have made the comment that you could hear a pin drop.

William was eventually given back to the state and spent much of his life in and out of jail. We have not heard anything of him in over a decade. My oldest brother was shot five times and killed in 2000, my senior year of high school. My Second oldest sister, after an attempted suicide from hearing voices, finally got the help and medication that she most likely needed her whole life. My oldest sister moved on and had her own family.

I give this history to bring and give this written perspective a background. This unrest and lack of development at key stages in life led me to believe certain things about myself. I believed that I could not rely on people, that I had to make my own way. I used my two older brothers as my examples of what I did not want to be. They made choices that brought them to places where they weren't around the best people. I did not want this for myself. I had a father who I know had love for me, but again, showed no interest in me aside from seeing me have a good education. I am grateful for that choice he made but I believed I was on my own and that I could not model my life with him as my example of what I felt a father was or needed to be. I made my way through school and college, making safe choices, and while disruptive at times and a clown in class, I overall made good choices that brought me a college degree. Those missed stages of development in my life had not fully taken its toll on me. I went through childhood and adolescence not knowing who I was, I had no identity. I hung out with White kids, but did I feel White? No. I looked different. By the time I got into high school it was 90% Black. Did I care that it was a predominantly Black school? No. Again, I had no idea who I was and ended up bouncing around in different groups, trying to find who I was on my own. I had no man to show me the way. I felt most accepted by Hispanics because I resembled a person of Dominican heritage. I fell into this persona so much so that I hung a Dominican flag in my room. After this persona lost its mask, I hung out with a friend of mine at that time who was half Korean. We had so much in common with not feeling that we belonged to either of the communities that we were half of. He was half Black and Korean. For years, I hung out with him and his friends, mostly Korean. Even then, I did not feel like I belonged. And as the years went on, I felt more and more on the outs, as I could see him falling into and being accepted more into the Korean community. I could not join him in that part of his journey. So again, I was left without an identity and on my own. I felt this way, whether it was right or wrong; it was my perspective and my beliefs, no matter how false they might have been.

I went on my own from there. I bounced around religions and spiritual practices, mostly shamanism. I was searching for myself and wanted to find myself. I could not see myself as Black or White and didn't feel I belonged anywhere. I went into my dreams as they started to resurface. This is when the ride really began.

More and more intense dreams started, and the images during the day became much more intense as well. The brave pretense that I had made it and got through my lacking childhood and won began to breakdown. More anger entered that I could not turn away with internal talk of better things to come. As more and more of my attempts to create a life for myself in sports and in work and life failed me. The "next" thing (really a distraction) was not there for me to work toward, and I could not hold an idea of how it would end up for me.

After much denial of where I was in life, several more failed attempts at trying to distract from dreams and daytime internal feelings that had always been there, and a failed shotgun marriage, I had a choice to make again in my life. I could continue this way of being, or I could start doing the work I needed to do to heal and move on in my life.

This choice did not come easy and came with a tremendous amount of pain and hard honesty with myself on who I had become. I started my journey going to a treatment center in New Mexico for a month to face my trauma and PTSD. I did not really believe it; however, I went through the motions, but felt it wasn't for me. Remember, Brian, you beat this, you won. I was in denial. I went into anger next. The anger had been there through periods of my life, as was denial. The anger would be triggered by many things, feeling left out, not heard, not appreciated for what I brought or offered. The kindness I displayed at times I felt was not seen. These are just a few examples, but the outside world around me and those closest to me would say that they believed that I felt that the world "owed" me. They were right, I did feel that I was owed, that I deserved to be seen, that my story had value. I'd had my childhood and stages of development and basic human dignity striped from me. I felt that no one in my family nor friend circle saw my struggle nor appreciated my life's story of what I shared. They would only respond with 'Brian or UB (Uncle Brian) is in one of his moods.' Moods that I learned was the way to handle things as a child. I believed that they thought it wasn't "that bad" "others have far less than we do." "Be grateful for what you have." Those comments and unsaid feelings made me angrier and at the same time made me think that maybe they were right, and caused me to feel ashamed of who I was and guilty for the choices I made as a kid and young adult to shield myself in an attempt to better my life. This is a mindset that I circled around in for a long time.

At the mid-point of this journey, I was angry still and felt that I was wronged, and yes, that I was owed for having my childhood taken. I had spent at that point $25k of my own money to pursue the healing I needed. I received no help from insurance through the Affordable Care Act. I reached out to several attorney's after reading a story of woman in Seattle who had a similar childhood as I and received a large settlement in the millions from the state for her experience in their foster care. Each conversation ended with 'I cannot help you.' The last Maryland attorney I spoke to explained that he takes my type of cases for free. He then explained that unfortunately I was ten years too late. Maryland had changed their laws in regard to liability for foster care abuse and that cases were needing to be brought to the courts by the age of twenty-five. Ten years too late. I asked him in complete anger, what would happen to me if I went out and did those things to another person that had happened to me? His response? "You would spend the rest of your life in jail." He advised that I write a letter to the state of Maryland about my experience in their foster care but to write in when I am not longer in the place of anger I was in. It took me six months to get to that space. I wrote a very well thought out four-page letter to the foster care system in PG county and to offices in Baltimore. After having to resend it two times, I finally received my answer from them. They said, "thank you for sharing your experience, this will go a long way to teaching our social workers in the foster care system." Did I even get an apology? No, not in one sentence did they apologize and take some responsibility for the torture I had gone through. I was in anger for a very long time after this. What had that stripped from me; experience wise, development wise, who would I be now if I'd had a normal childhood? All these types of questions were going through my mind constantly as I was still having dreams and day flashbacks.

I still had no identity settled and would still need to make my own way through my healing. I could not rely on the state of Maryland to take responsibility for what happened, and I certainly could not expect there to be any help with expenses for this journey. I made the choice that I would have to continue if I wanted to move on and have a better quality of life.

During this whole time, I was seeing my therapist and at times fully listening to what she had to say but was still stuck in my old way of being, believing that I had the answers and that I could get myself through and out.

Still not having an identity, I began to experience racial issues again at work. The last time I had an experience up to this point was when I was in Florida and at a friend's bachelor's party. He pulled me aside and told me that a friend of his present at the party had asked Tripp why he invited niggers to his party. Tripp told me this because that individual had been talking to me for most of the night, and Tripp did not want me to be around him. I thought the whole time I was being accepted by the group, a White group. I left the party because of how much hurt I was feeling inside and cried on my way home, driving more than slightly inebriated. I pulled up to my apartment on the south side of Jacksonville Florida. I got out of my car and then heard immediately, "Hey, White boy, hey, White boy." I was ignoring the four of them after turning around once. As I got to my front door, I heard for the last time, "Hey, you, fucking White boy," as they laughed hysterically. They were Black.

At work, I was told that I was the master's son. When I responded back with confusion, this older Black woman then explained to me that if it were slavery times, I would be in the house with the master. This was said in front of another Black person who I thought was my friend. The friend later denied that this took place. Again hurt, why did she lie to me about what was said to me? I let that go, still not knowing how I felt, but it was growing.

A few months later, a team was needing to be made up of at least 3 Black people. I was one of the people chosen for this role. While at the table, one of the other Black people said to the team leader that they needed to go back and get another Black person because they only had 2.5 Black people. Counting me only as half a Black person. I responded candidly at this point with "Oh, that's right, I'm not Black." My anger with this racial experience was building in me. Again, just a few months later, while at this place of work, I was working with two Black people and was sitting in the back of the car. Somehow they got on the topic of slavery. I had chimed in with some factual knowledge that I had about slavery, and after a few moments of silence, they both said, "Oh, that's right, Brian, you wouldn't be out in the fields with us and the rest of the slaves, you would be in the house with the master."

About half a year later, I was on the subway for work and sat down in front of two Black girls. The train was crowded, and that seat was available. As the train started moving, I heard them describe a bi-racial person who fit my description—curly hair, light skin, and green eyes. They talked about how they think they are so privileged. That they were not really Black and that they are "fucking White." They then went into how proud they are of being Black and that they would not want to be "fucking White bitches." Even though one of them had "blonde" hair. I realized at some point that their conversation was directed at me. This time, I didn't feel angry or let down on the outside. It made me realize that just because I sat in front of them, they didn't like that. That I did that because in some way I felt entitled to simply take a seat in front of them on a crowded train. I did not feel anger anymore, I felt sad for them and beyond where they were stuck. They were stuck in what I had been working to pull myself through. A victim mindset.

I went back to all the recent racial struggles I had experienced up to that point, and I asked myself, why have I been pushed out, considered separate, and not a part of? The answer was that part of my reflection is that of a White person, of which they feel resentment toward, and with some hate. I realized what they are carrying is no different than what I was carrying toward all those people in the foster care home, Maryland's Social Services, and some people in my family who hurt me. A victim mindset. Though I had not placed a race on it, as I have never carried any resentment toward someone's color, I did feel that I was owed, I was angry, hurt, not seen, not heard, treated as less, passed up, damaged in some way.

As I continue on my journey of healing, acceptance of what happened to me, and the gifts received, the love I have come to feel and allow in, I realized that I had to make a choice to let all of it go. That I had to make the choice to want something better for my life, that I wanted to be free in my mind from what happened and not be held prisoner by it. I also realized that I had expected this freedom to be handed to me in some monetary and verbal form, because I deserved it for all that I went through. These were needed in order for me to receive "justice." Oh, I so desperately wanted justice for the all the wrong that was directly inflicted on me. At some point, I chose to see that life does not work like that. That we are dealt the hands that we are dealt. Whether we deserve them or not, whether one person or group is wrong or right, we as an individual have the power to choose differently. We can allow it to control our lives, to define who we are, where we will and can go, and the quality of our lives. I have chosen to forgive myself of the choices I made that pushed good people away from me, who did nothing to me, but who I felt slighted by. I chose to let go of my guilt, to let go of the belief that I do not know who I am and that I am alone and lost.

I am Brian S., a human being who can be described as bi-racial but not defined by it, who has a gift of deep understanding of the struggles of others, compassion for those struggles, and none-judgment of their journey. I have let go of the idea that money will provide healing and safety for me. I was being met with blocks and ceilings in my work life that I could not navigate around or through, so I have chosen to walk away from a $100k a year job to pursue my master's degree in social work in order for me to learn another way of being. To learn more about myself, to continue to heal while doing my best to make a difference in others' lives by being an example of someone who has gone through a wide range of hurts and struggles and has made choices that do not leave me stuck in a self-destructive mindset. To show that a person facing multiple racial discriminations, a person who had no idea who they were or where they belonged has the right, free will, and ability to make a different choice for themselves. That their choice can define them, not their race, childhood deficiencies, or losses. They are not damaged.

In making that choice to let go and pursue better paths and quality of life, those people who will help you will be sent and will walk a part of your journey with you to help and to be helped, but you have to be in the right place and mind to receive this. It has taken me close to fifteen years to get to this place in my journey of healing and understanding of my life, and I still have much to understand and learn. If it has taken me fifteen years and there is still more to do, how can I expect anyone outside myself and those experiences to fully understand me or know the feelings that go along with them? I cannot expect that. All I can ask is an ear to listen and some words of advice, the rest I must do internally and with my ability to choose better.

I am never a token unless you see me smoking a Hookah. I am in no one's box or house unless I choose to be. I am a free thinking free human being who can make positive or negative choices as I see fit. I choose a positive life, a quality life that provides help to the communities that I will support and the family that I will create. All of this requires me to make good choices for myself, none of that can be handed or given to me by anyone else or state.

I want to take a moment to walk through an imagination with you. Imagine YOU, not anyone else, not even a family member, but you. Imagine images carried with you of hunger that would make you eat paper, finding a window to feel the sun and then having that taken away only to sit in a cage. Imagine not knowing from where or when you would feel pain but knowing it would come. Imagine having images of sex before you knew what sex was, before knowing it was wrong and before knowing it wasn't something you wanted to do. Imagine you were taken out of that, finding a place where it all stopped in the matter of a day. Imagine wondering how long that would be, was it permanent, was it real, or would it be taken away like your window? Imagine it starting all over again; the pain, the unwanted moments of sexual acts. Imagine the questions and stories you would tell yourself. That you remember questioning how long it would last, the trick. Imagine the closest person you had through all of these images shut you out and left. You are alone now. Imagine lying to yourself and creating a world that only you could be in. Only allowing those in for the moments you wanted to dip your toes in another experience, only to go back to that bubble because you knew it would end too. Imagine this story you told yourself was an agreement you made to never show weakness, lying to yourself because you felt the fear every day, not knowing the what or when but knowing it would come. You must imagine strength now to believe in not going back, but never believing that. Imagine running from yourself because the images would come if you didn't. Imagine needing to be something other than yourself and then losing the thought of yourself when your innocence made you run away. Imagine how easy the anger would creep and seep into you now. Imagine the confusion you have even now in imagining all of this. How that confusion doesn't allow you to turn to anyone because you can't explain, you don't have the words, only the image, and no one to understand you. You are alone. You can't stay here, you see another image, you see those around you making choices that you could see were made by the same feelings in you, images of the pain that resides in you. You don't want to be that. What to do, how to be, confusion, and another lie. You can be an image that would allow you to navigate the world you walk through without anyone knowing what the feeling is inside. Imagine this created image bringing you fun and friends, but no one gets in, no one sees you or can feel you. You do not need anyone now, and you are alone, the lie. Imagine how confused you are right NOW and how you need to deny to keep going. Who are you? Imagine the images of the pain and the hurt, the images of having everything taken from you, how they are with you every day and many nights. They are getting too close; you have to run again. Imagine creating another image and then, the pain fades.

It is a lot of imagining, but now imagine how tired you feel. Imagine the question of can you keep going, but you must so those closest can't see you, they never talked to you anyway, you are alone. Imagine questioning did they believe you, do you believe yourself now, confusion. Who are you, no one showed you, remember you imagined you are alone? Imagine you don't know love now because it has been so long since your innocence, but you find a way to feel good and to be in control, and for a brief moment, you are not alone in your imagination, not confused nor tired. You can imagine easily now, with all the practice, all sorts of things, and alone you practice sex. Now you have found a way to feel how you feel and it's easy to keep from everyone, you can still navigate the world with how you need to feel and not destroy it like the others had, and no one will know. Imagine that carrying you for so long, but then wanting love you don't know, you become tired again and no longer want to be, no longer wanting to BE here.

My son, I am God, creator of all things, why do you doubt me? My son, I am God, creator of all things, why do you doubt me? My son, I am God, creator of all things, why do you doubt me? Imagine traveling to three worlds, a world of vast oceans, a world of endless Deserts, and a world of great mountains, alone but not alone. A moment of understanding, that when physically alone we are not alone, even in a vast desert. In all this confusion, the lost feeling you feel right now after imagining so much, you realize the biggest and most damaging impact of life was the beginning lie, the first lie, when you told yourself that you are alone.

I want you to imagine one last time, in a different way, from another angle, on the other side of the room. Look back and imagine how you could not have been alone and protected your mind. You could not have because you did not know how. Look and see that even amongst all the pain and hurt, you still were able to look out the window and see light and find joy. See the strength you had that was just there, a strength that had never been shown nor practiced. I was speaking to you then, I never stopped speaking to you. I was beside you the entire time. That was not your voice you heard but mine. I reminded you at night, I had to because you blocked me and questioned me during the day. You could not hear me. I sent you signs of heart when you needed, shielded you from injury. I spoke to you through them. The power I gave your heart was never gone, was never taken from you. You are my MATI in this world, and that is my gift to you. I need you to listen to me now, I need you to trust me now more than ever. I need you. You have been asking me and questioning why I stopped speaking through dreams. I want to tell you. I no longer needed to because you started listening to me. The music opened your heart to me again. I used it to speak to you, MATI, but you had to choose to. There is still much doubt in you now, let me guide you through. The feeling you have that you call "sit back" is me. I love you, son, and I forgive you.

I wrote a lot about what was done to me, what I went through, and who did those things to me. I wrote a lot about the narrative I took from those experiences, the false beliefs in myself, the unhealthy view I carried, about people, even those close to me, those who had never done anything to me but being their own person who went through their own hurts and difficulties. I continued to write about my anger, my feeling of being owed for what was taken away from me and the justice that was needing to be served.

I carried these ideas of myself, the world and those resentments that came from my mentality for most of my life. It brought me a lot of pain, setbacks in my carrier, lost and broken relationships. I asked "why?" all the time. The question would never leave. Why were these things done to me? Why did I deserve to go through all of that? Why would people do those things to a child? Why did they get away with it? Why was no one there to save and protect my brother and I? I never received an answer to this, through all my anger and pain, the answer to those questions never fell on me. I searched and searched, going to South America to take a "medicine" that was to bring healing and answers to questions had. I gave so much power away to so-called healers and medicine men. Searching for my answer and to learn if I was damaged, as I thought my entire life. The "medicine" brought me no answer, only brought me good people who I moved away from because I was stuck in my questioning and not seeing. I walked through darkness, loneliness, sadness, and passive suicidal thoughts of not wanting to be "here" anymore but to be in a better place, a quiet place, and to be at peace from the struggle of confusion. It was a never-ending circle of excitement of starting a path to find answers and a way out, only to end with the pain of the letdown that followed.

The answer to the question "why?" is—we can never know why people severely hurt others. We can never know why, because we are not God and cannot completely know how people work, what pathways were created from their own tragic experiences, how the events of their life molded them, their thoughts, their beliefs about themselves, their place in the world and how they interact with that world. We can judge them to satisfy our needs. Some of us get the opportunity to face and ask those who have done us wrong, why? Why they did what they did, for our closure. They can give their answer, but even those answers are skewed by their molded view of the world around themselves. They cannot fully understand their actions and deeds and cannot therefore give you that answer. They can find forgiveness for their actions, and in that; give you an apology. You can make your own choice in what you want to accept and not from that apology, but you cannot know why.

I want to write about another question to ask from tragic events that happen in life, after we have grieved them. I want to ask, what was given in that moment or those moments, if the events were more than once? With my experience, I want to look back and see my mother. What did my mother bring to me? She brought me another life filled with more opportunity, things that she could not supply for me. No one is guaranteed an easy path, but her intention was to give me another way. She saw that if she kept me, the cycle of poverty would continue. For her difficult choice to give up her children, I can say thank you for wanting a better way for us, no matter what you said or wanted for yourself in that moment you let us go. To the foster care family, I can see what you brought me. You brought me a lot of pain, a lot of pain, but in that pain, brought me closer to God, more than anyone on this planet could have done. Your actions brought God, who walked with me, protecting me. He shielded my mind until a time I could handle it. Him protecting my mind and my heart allowed me to work for a better life. That protection kept me from being so far gone after what happened that I couldn't eventually find my way back. You brought me an internal strength that reaches far beyond me and affects others. Like all superheroes, you must go through struggles and tragedies to gain your powers. You were the ones who created the environment for me to receive and later see my powers. You did not take them away. To Dad, you brought me an understanding of what a father should be. You made me realize now how desperately I wanted a father, even though I told myself I did not. Now I can be that father and know how important that is in a child's life. To my mother, you brought me love, the deepest of compassion, commitment, and the kind of strength that I would not see until much later in life. The strength to pick myself up and continue to move forward even in the face of difficulties and struggles, to never give up. You made sure that I received what I needed to succeed in life. To my oldest sister, you brought me joy, laughter, and a feeling of belonging and acceptance. To my oldest brother you taught me that we are never guaranteed a smooth ride, that we are not saved from going through hard and hurtful events only once in our life. You enabled me to have a deeper connection with God and the spirit world. From your visits and asking of forgiveness, I forgive you now. To my second oldest sister, you taught me much later in life how to forgive. Your forgiveness of me allowed me the time to heal and to see your gentleness, which broke down the walls I built up around me to keep me from you. Now I see you were just acting out from the pain you too felt inside. I forgive you and thank you for that. To William, you walked with me through our beginning. Though we never walked together in our lives again, I am grateful for that first walk together, the closeness and the friend I had through it all.

To Alana, you brought me the understanding that I am always worthy of Love. That I am someone of value and who has many gifts to share. You remind me of this by your kind words and actions toward me every day. You taught me to see the gifts of others as well. That not everyone is out to get me or to take from me. To Halle, you taught me that no matter how far we stray from our path, we can always find our way back and find our purpose in this life. Through your patience and care, you taught me how to begin to trust again. Showing me that I am not alone in the journey I am walking in this world. Thank you.

So much of my time spent was seeing what I was without, what I thought was taken away from me. I was not able to see the gifts that come with my experiences. I am not alone in those takeaways. I had to let go of the idea that I am a victim. I needed to choose to open myself up and feel worthy of more in this life. I no longer need the "Why," because I see the gift.

Author's Notes

It is not your fault that you've been through traumatic situations in your life, but it is for damn sure your responsibility to figure out how to take that pain and how to overcome that and build a happy life for yourself.
~ Will Smith

The pain and hurtful experiences that we go through in life are real! It doesn't matter how little, how often, or how devasting it was; it happened! However, it's a choice of what we do with that pain that makes us grow, get stronger, and separates us from the rest. It the difference between two fighters, one who gets hit and stays down, or the other who gets up, no matter how many times they get knocked to the ground. These are the people who look life straight in the eyes with pain and blood leaking from their body and ask "Is that all you got!"

In the forging of a Samurai sword, two types of metals are used. One metal is very hard and allows for a razor-sharp edge.

The other one is very tough and allows for shock absorption. These two metals are heated intensely then hammered flat and folded over and over again. This process creates layers into the sword, it makes it unique, strong, valuable, and worthy!

This is how most of us are forged in our lives! We've been torched, beaten, and have layers of negativity and abuse folded into our lives! Like the Samurai sword, these things are what makes it so strong, durable, and valuable.

Like the master whom this powerful weapon is made for, we are the masters in our own life, but if we don't use the sword, we will never win the battles we were destined to fight.

> *"Good is fitting in, great is fitting out."*
> *~Ray Lewis*

Racism is real. No matter what color you are, somewhere and someone will not like you! I've learned throughout my life that trying to fit in is the hardest thing to do, it's like trying to put a square in a circle, forgetting you have edges. None of us are perfect, and we all have flaws. Our lives, and life in general, is beautiful because of these things, only if we choose to accept them!

We get in life what we expect, and many times; that could be good or bad, so if bad things persist, you know where it's coming from, and if you want better, expect more for yourself, and for others.

I've learned to change my story from devastation, defeat, and lack of support, for the reason why I wasn't succeeding. My new story, now; because of the devastation, defeat, and lack of support, is the reason why I must and will succeed. I've also learned to change my prayers; I no longer ask God for wealth and happiness. I now ask God to allow me to use all of the gifts and talents that HE'S put in me. To use them and create the wealth and happiness that I expect in life, and help others do the same!

"So do not fear, for I am with you; do not be dismayed,
for I am your God. I will strengthen you and help you;
I will uphold you with my righteous right hand."
Isaiah 41:10 (NIV)

God has an amazing way of being where we think He is not! It's usually in our deepest and darkest moments that God truly reveals His presence in our lives. Don't lose faith, don't give up, fight the good fight, and prevail in His name!

CHAPTER 18

The Crossroads

Journal Entry

Monday 10/22/12 4:39pm

I think after living three lives, I'd be ready to die. Recently, I feel like I've been pulled between wanting to live a life dedicated to service and a life lived for art. Being in this hotel surrounded by all these books has reminded me how much I love beauty, but having grown up overseas and taking a tour of the local clinic here and what not, I am constantly aware of the immediate need surrounding me. I picked up a book off the shelf earlier this morn- ing called "A Little Treasure of Modern Poetry" and opened it to a random page, and there I read the poem "I Died for Beauty" by Emily Dickinson, in which she died for beauty but the person next to her died for truth, and it made me wonder what I wanted to live for. I think this is why I have such a hard time making up my mind about my major, because what I want to do with my life and what I love don't line up. And maybe it's because the life I had wanted before wasn't actually what I had wanted but what I'd known. Maybe my mind chose a life of service because, as of *now, my skills are definitely NOT up to par to excel in any of the arts. So, as not to disappoint, it chose the second-rate life that it knew I could attain and still feel accomplished with. I know the arts (writing, drawing, dancing) can always be a hobby, but I hate doing anything half-heartedly, and I feel like with the two lives I am currently torn between, it would be hard to find a compromise that would do either justice. Both take time. So much time. Hence, I think after having lived three lives, I would be ready to die. Because even if I sectioned off my life to where I have ten years to traveling, ten years to service, and yet another ten purely to art, I would be torn between the worlds, never fully content with one. I think there would always be a part of me that would be longing for the other. And then there is the question that must be asked. Is it too late for me to live for art? Seeing that I am already twenty-one and I do not consider myself an artist of any sorts, I've never dabbled in dance, and I believe that I have a little bit of a poet in me but she still needs much work and refining to be done before she can emerge and I can truly, comfortably, call myself a poet. And maybe this is just me being whimsical and dreamy, looking to the future with rose tinted glasses, but reality has yet to set in, and until then; I will dream big, because I can't stand the thought of simply being average. In my life, I **will** be anything but that.*

My name is Hannah P., and this is my story.

I won my race in the shoes of my mother and father. For the last forty years, my parents have worked overseas with NGOs in community development. They are some of the most passionate, loving people I know. Growing up overseas,

I saw the ardent fire they had for their work. They live a life of service, working on development projects, primarily in South East Asia. For a long time, I saw how alive they were through their relationship with God and their work He had given a gift and passion for. I wanted to have that same passion for work in my life. I wanted to find my calling. I was acutely aware for the needs of the world and wanted to help. I wanted to feel alive with the same passion I saw in my parents. I took a gap year, volunteered on a medical ship, and decided I was going to be a nurse. I did not want to be in a hospital. I wanted to work in disaster zones overseas as a relief worker. I figured whatever I did, it would be helpful to have nursing in my back pocket to whip out at a moment's notice. Or, for starters, it would be my ticket to get myself overseas again after college. I thought, if not me, then who? Who would help the world in desperate need of help? I felt the weight on my shoulders, and reasoned any other life would be a selfish life.

The first few years of college came and went. Turns out, I hated going to my nursing classes. I didn't feel alive. I didn't feel passionate about the course content. I didn't know what to do. I've come to realize I am a person who is great at looking at the big picture but creating tangible steps to live day to day life and move forward achieving life goals is a weakness. I am so grateful I went to a small college where I had mentors who were able to help me along the way, and my parents who were fully supportive.

At my university, one of the core requirements to graduate was a study abroad. I went to South Africa and Lesotho the fall of my junior year. It was then I wrote the journal entry above.

We had visited clinics for HIV patient care, and other rural clinics with only a handful of nurses and one or two doctors serving thousands of patients. I saw places where I could fill the need for help everywhere. I was torn. My indecision was making me freeze. I was sitting in small a boutique hotel in the middle of a small town in South Africa. The owner was passionate about books and records, and in every hallway and room of the hotel shelves from floor to ceiling were filled with books. I sat scribbling away in my journal, searching for answers. I was in despair. How could I justify a life of anything but service when I was so acutely aware of the need I was surrounded by in the world?

At the height of my anxiety, my iPod started to ring. My parents were trying to Skype me. I picked up. "Hannah, we just got a call from your school's registrar office. They said you aren't signed up for any classes next semester. What's going on?" I told them I was torn. I didn't love nursing and I wasn't happy, but I didn't know if I should push on or switch majors. I remember saying, "but what if it's the wrong decision?" and then, as clear and calm as day, my father said, "Hannah, it's America, you can always switch back." He added, "It might take you longer, but if you try it and it's not for you, you can always switch back." And just like that, the huge weight began to lift off my shoulders. They talked me through some more concerns and worries I had. They told me God has given us all different gifts and passions, and it's through harnessing and refining those gifts that God ignites a passion and uses us to help others in life. Looking back, I can see so many moments that should have been epiphanies steering me toward my gifts and passions. How I wrote poems and short stories, often in secret, in my room when I was very young, or when I was in high school, the only class I stayed up all night for was my writing class. I didn't have to, but I was excited about the writing assignment, and when we wrote monologues to turn in, I was so full of ideas I wrote six. I also realized I've always been drawn to older people for mentorship. It's something I've truly cherished throughout my life. I remember stepping into a professor's office once, she was a professor of sociology and had spent many years working with HIV/AIDs programs in South Africa. I asked her about my major and what I should do. She said, "if you can push through, do it, but if you feel like it's going to be the death of you, switch." I switched my major to writing. It was the right decision.

I didn't know it when I was on the phone with my parents, but they were nervous and wondered what someone could do with a writing degree. They worried I would have a hard time finding a job after graduating. They didn't know God was using them to speak truth into my life.

I graduated from college, and for the first few months, I worked as a nanny and at a coffee shop. I even had a part time gig cat-sitting. A coworker's husband at the coffee shop worked as Diplomatic Security Agent. She knew their training facility was hiring program coordinators, and she immediately thought of me because I lived and grew up overseas, and the program was working with Foreign Service Officers living and working overseas coming for training. I applied and got the job. I have worked for Diplomatic Security as a contractor for the last five years. I've written a few magazine articles and use my writing in my work all the time. It's been eight years since the journal entry. I recently applied to be a Diplomatic Security Agent. I've made it to the final selection round but am waiting for an interview date to be set. In the future, I want to continue working toward a long-term goal of teaching at a collegiate level as a professor. I want to teach writing and help mentor a young generation by helping them find their passions. I've realized I am passionate about seeing others come alive. In the future, I hope I can do what my parents and other mentors did for me and help others find their passions and gifts in life.

Dear Mom and Dad,

Thank you for living your life to the fullest, full of passion and with God's light in it every day. It hasn't always been the easiest path, but I look up to you every single day. You are and have always been role models for me. Through your lives, you have shown me what it means to live a life on fire for God, and what it means to use your passions and gifts for good. I thank God all the time for being born into your family. I loved growing up overseas and am forever thankful you listened to God's call for your life. I love you with all my heart and am so thankful I've had your full support and listening ear through all the decisions in my life. Thank you for everything.

Your loving daughter,

Hannah

Author's Notes,

*"It's not who you are that holds you back,
it's who you think you're not."*
~ Gina Milicia

Many times, in our lives we get torn between who we are, and who we're capable of becoming! It's our choice to be the best version of ourselves! However, the best version of us is usually the hardest to reach. Knowing that this person exists sometimes put so much pressure on us, because deep down, we know that we're nowhere close to becoming them!

We have many different paths that we can take in life, but only one of them is truly meant for us!

"The Lord said to her in reply, "Martha, Martha, you are anxious and worried about many things. There is need of only one thing. Mary has chosen the better part and it will not be taken from her."
Luke 10:41-42

It's easy to walk the path that others have traveled before, because all you have to do is follow. What most people don't want to do is create their own path to a destination that no one has ever been before. It's often scary to go off a path that's already made, it's scary following your dreams, goals, and true passions in life!

"Do not go where the path may lead,

go instead where there is no path and leave a trail."
~Ralph Waldo Emerson

When we are stuck in life, many times God finds a way to comfort us with His words and guidance! It may not come directly from Him, but He will send it from a parent, a friend, or even on the television. No matter what method God chooses, it's always clear to us in the moment. The only issue is if we choose to listen and take action. He is always there for us, if we only ask Him to be.

Serving others in life is one of the greatest privileges and most fulfilling things that any human being can do, especially if they're doing it for God! We've all been given a gift to bring to this world, many of us either don't know what that gift is or how to use it, and some people don't believe it's popular enough to make a difference and money!

No matter what your gift is, know that it's more than good enough, God put it in you to bring it forth to the world for a reason. It's up to us to figure out how to use it for a greater purpose, and when we do this, God will always create the way for it to reward us!

I'm reminded of a story in the book of Matthew in the bible.

"A Master gives three of his servants each a certain amount of money and tells them to do good with it. On returning, he asks the servants what did you do with my money. Two of them doubled their share, and one hid his and gave it back to the master just as he received it out of fear of losing it. The master was proud, and

gave more responsibility to the ones who used the money well, and the one who hid the money, it was taken away and given to the servants who used the money well."

There is more to this story, however, I believe if we don't use the gifts that we've been given, we'll have a hard time explaining to God when we die that we allowed fear to stop us from using them!

"In the Beginning was the Word, and the Word was with God, and the Word was God." John 1:1 NIV

The gift to write, the ability to create in your mind and transfer it on paper for others to be inspired is amazing. The words that God has put inside of these special people has the ability to touch and serve millions! Allow your light to shine more in this world, because it's needed more than we can imagine! Bless this world with your gift from God. Serve others with the art of capturing, love, life, passions, inspiration, and adventure in the words you put on paper! The ability to communicate with people by writing is truly serving, and painting a masterpiece in the minds and heart of others, is truly giving this world a gift from God!

"Don't ask yourself what the world needs. Ask yourself what makes you come alive, and go do that, because what the world needs is people who have come alive."
~Howard Thurman

CHAPTER 19

Strength of a Mother

I watched as my mother struggled to raise two kids, being a single mother. We didn't have much growing up, but my Mother always ensured we had wonderful Holidays, dinner on the table, clothes on our back, healthy, and had a good relationship with God.

I'm Sean F, and this is my story.

I won my race in the shoes of my Mother.

My Mother is a strong-minded person, loving, and fair. She tried her best to raise a son and daughter while working full time and going to school as a single mother. I started hanging around the wrong people, did the bare minimum to get by in school, and was headed down the wrong road. Friends around me were dying, getting locked up, or were headed deeper down the road in which I never wanted to visit.

I didn't want to go down the same path as my other friends, and I realized that my mother was doing the best that she could for our family. I saw my mother crying and praying for me to be better, I wanted to do more for my mother, who sacrificed everything for my sister and me.

I needed to get away from the demons around me, so I graduated high school and I joined the Army. Today, after serving twenty years in the Army, I've achieved a high rank with many awards and experiences. I have a wonderful family of my own, a beautiful wife, and two wonderful sons. I ensure my family lives well and never has to experience the hardships we went through, and ensuring they have all opportunities life has to offer. We continue to grow as a family, and I continue to instill the same qualities in my children to ensure they are ready for the world.

My mother would always say to keep your head up and always try your best in everything you do. She always ensured we displayed manners and appreciation. She always ensured we understood nothing was free in life and to work hard. Living in small apartments, not having nice clothes or things, my Mother always ensured we had dinner on the table. Although we would have qualified, she never accepted anything free, (i.e., food stamps, etc.) and showed us hard work pays off. She always reminded us how much we were loved by her and God. She instilled God, manners, a hardworking attitude, respect, compassion, and empathy. I remember a few Thanksgivings we would invite a homeless person to our home for Thanksgiving Dinner. She would help my little sister and I understand that life can be challenging and difficult, but to never quit. Have compassion for others and give a leaning hand. Always keep your head up, pray, and do your very best at everything you do, and it will pay off. She taught us to be appreciative of what we have, because things can always be worse. Today, both my sister and I are very well off, my mother remarried and is also doing well. I truly believe the hardships we went through in life and everything she instilled in us helped us to be prepared for the real world. She helped shaped me as a young man and as a good citizen, which has helped me accomplish what I have today. I never want my children to live the way we did, but also want to ensure they are appreciative everything God and my wife and I provide. I want to ensure they work hard, are compassionate, have a good relationship with God, and are good people.

Thank you for never giving up on me, God truly blessed me with a mother like you who never gave up on me, I wouldn't be where I am in life today without your love.

Author's notes,
"She was unstoppable, not because she
did not have failures or doubts.
But because she continued on despite them."
~Beau Taplin – Unstoppable

The strength that women possess is so amazing. They have an unlimited source of it because, built within their DNA is the greatest power of all; "LOVE." It's the one thing that if we can all remember that we have, it would give us the fighting spirit of never giving up. It's the thing that can change lives, create happiness, bring world peace, and change this world. It's a small word, that has a gigantic impact when it strikes!

"Don't raise your kids to have more than you had, raise
them to be more than you were." ~ Unknown

Being a parent becomes harder every generation. We want to have our children see and experience the same hardship we endured because it built us into who we are today. The hard part though, is even though some of those lessons are truly important, and should be continued, we must understand that the generation that they're growing up in isn't ours. We must also know that the people we became, isn't who we should want them to become!

Giving children the best that we can is truly loving them more than we were ever loved. Loving is understanding them, that they have their own path to take in life. Loving them is providing a safe and healthy environment for them to grow and develop into who God intended them to be.

*"Speak to your children as if they are the wisest,
kindest, most beautiful and magical humans on earth,
for what they believe is what they will become."*
~Brooke Hampton

CHAPTER 20

Fighting Spirit

My parents divorced when I was nine years old. My father did not fight for custody, and I was powerless to have any say at such a young age. I endured physical, mental, emotional, and financial abuse at the hands of my Narcissistic Personality Disordered mother. My father was absent. He struggled with his own alcoholic demons. I was treated as a lesser-than by my mother but was required to oversee my three younger siblings.

I'm Molly, and this is my story. I won my race in the shoes of my mentor, Melissa.

Melissa is a soul-doctor. Her firm, fair, and consistent presence allows people to be vulnerable, accountable, courageous, and to heal. She is passionate and strong minded but is not afraid to admit her mistakes and make amends when required. I was lost. After doing all the "right things" per my mother's expectations (I graduated college), I did not know who I was or what to do. I had so much learned helplessness, that I was starting to consume alcohol more frequently (not in crazy amounts, but enough to scare me!). I was lost without someone to tell me what to do, when to do it, and how to do it. I was depressed and had thoughts of dying.

I did not really want to die. I had a good life with a loving and supportive husband. I went to Melissa because I was desperate to tell someone about the thoughts in my head. I was scared. She shared her story with me, and I found someone with a very similar history, and suddenly the world was not such a lonely, scary, bleak place. She guided me toward therapy and a check in with a medical professional who specialized in mental health concerns. She taught me that "everything happens for a reason; it is just none of our business," and she allowed me to challenge her (a strong woman) when I felt wronged and taught me I would not be physically, mentally, or emotionally retaliated against for doing so. She taught me how to be kinder to myself and that seeking professional help was very much okay!

Over time, I got better. I went for my master's degree and became a dually licensed mental health and addiction counselor. I have two beautiful children and a growing private practice. My mental health is the best it has ever been, and each day I learn and grow! I am also fifteen years into my recovery journey, the last three of which have been from sugar/processed foods which kept me stuck in the sick cycle with my family of origin.

Melissa would always say, "Everything happens for a reason—it isn't your business" she also said, "You are NOT Jesus Christ, get off the cross." These are hugely important to me, as I tend to want to control all aspects of life, AND I am naturally inclined to play the martyr to get people to like me. She taught me that not everyone is going to like me, and that is okay!

Melissa,

Thank you for inviting me to your table. You saw something in me when I could see zero value in myself. You offered your hand and your heart and made me a chosen member of your family. Without you, I do not know where I would be today. I am a better wife, friend, mother, and sister because of how you showed up for me. You allowed me to be vulnerable and taught me that I do not have to be afraid of other women. You taught me how to be spiritual in a way that works for me. I am forever grateful and can never repay you. I hope to pay it forward and walk as authentically and truthfully through this life as you have shown me how to do. I hope to see you again in the next life, the eternal life. I hope our souls always find one another. You are my guiding star. More importantly, you are my sister. May Creator keep you on the road.

With love,

Molly

Author's Notes,

"Happiness is when you feel good about yourself without feeling the need for anyone else's approval."

~Jelly, designer, LifeHack

One of the things that truly hurts my heart is seeing parents who don't care for their children. There are so many people in this world who truly want to have children, but for some odd reason aren't able to have them.

I feel for people like that, especially when you know that they have so much love that they want to give!

In many ways it's easy to be upset when you see things like that. However, should we be upset? Do we have the right to be upset? Are we questioning God and the things that go on in life that we can't and will never have control over?

These are the questions that go on in my mind when you look at things from a different perspective. I'm starting to realize more these days that there aren't any mistakes in life, we just haven't discovered yet what the real purpose is behind what is happening in the moment!

"Life is simple. Everything happens for you, not to you.
Everything happens at exactly the right
moment, neither too soon nor too late.
You don't have to like it... it's just easier if you do"
~Byron Katie

Many people in this world struggle internally, with depression, anxiety, schizophrenia, PTSD, just to name a few of the many mental illnesses. The sad and scary part is there are so many people who try to live their lives with it and never seek help. It's embarrassing, what will others think of me, will I be accepted or thought of as a sick person? These are the thoughts that I truly believe torment so many people.

"Whether an illness affects your heart, your leg, or your brain, it's still an illness." ~ Michelle Obama

We don't have to go through difficulties that we face in our lives alone! This is one of the hardest things for many people to know and accept. The pride of needing to be strong or being that person others perceive we are sometimes stops us from seeking the help and assistance that we truly need!

No matter what or how we attained these types of illnesses; at war, inherited it from birth, or from a traumatic childhood experience. Just know this—we aren't alone in this battle! Don't go through it by yourself, seek the help that you need, that will give you the proper ammunitions to fight back and defeat this enemy!

"I think the first step is to understand that forgiveness does not exonerate the perpetrator. Forgiveness liberates the victim. It's a gift you give yourself." ~ T.D. Jakes

CHAPTER 21

Fear of Love

Life was great as a young teenager. I didn't have a worry in the world besides school, homework, and the next time I was going to play basketball with my friends. I remember the days of spending so much time with my parents traveling and attending different event around the area. Everything was great to a point where I didn't know the meaning of stress.

Then, everything had changed to where I didn't understand anything that was going on around me. My parents were always upset with each other, complaining about the simplest things, and it got to the point where they didn't want to be around each other. You can only image how this made me feel since we as a family were always close. At this point, my parents decided to part ways from each other and live separate lives. When this happened, I decided to go with my mother, because I felt she needed me.

My mother and I packed everything we owned in a 1989 Volvo 240DL and headed south to my grandmother's house. I didn't like the idea, but it was totally out of my control, and

I still couldn't comprehend what was happening at the time. I had mixed emotions because I loved my mother and farther dearly, and it was heartbreaking that we had to go through this. When we arrived at my grandmother's house, I was happy to see her, but I had to digest that I was going to be here for an unknown duration.

After moving and settling in, I had to attend summer school so I can pass to the next grade and get acclimated to my new environment. I was very nervous of this whole thing, because now I must make new friends, and that was a terrifying moment for me. Summer school wasn't too bad. Once the normal school year came around, I truly had a hard time. I was being bullied because they knew I wasn't from there, I looked different, and I talked differently than everyone else. It got to a point where my anger was getting the best of me, and I was almost getting into fights every week.

Eventually, my grades started to decline. At this point, my parents were no longer speaking to each other, and my dad and I grew apart to the point where he was no longer in my life. I became the man of the house at thirteen years of age. I made a promise to my mother that I was never going to leave her side.

As a young adult and through adulthood, due to the trauma that was caused by my parents' separation, I adopted the fear of failure. A fear to fail as a husband, followed by the fear to fail as a parent. I was too afraid to make the same mistakes my parents made. For nine years, I avoided relationships for this reason, when a friendship was flourishing and feelings started to deepen, my instinct to back away kicked in full force.

I became a twenty-five-year-old with no sense of belonging but with a desire to love and be loved. I was broken, and I did not know a way to overcome my fear.

At twenty-six, I met who is now my wife and mother of my beautiful daughter. I had prayed relentlessly to God to allow me to love. We reconnected unexpectedly and somehow; I knew this was it. We started attending church together and made the promise to make God the center of our relationship. We've been married for seven years and have a daughter now. My fear of failing was replaced by the feeling to protect and love my wife and daughter. I have learned that I can win races in the shoes God gave me, that my parent's mistakes and even my mistakes do not define me as a person, as a husband, and as a parent.

Twelve long years passed until my father and I reconnected. I missed out on a lot, and so did he, but our bond is stronger than ever, and I thank God every day for that. As for my mother, she also has rekindled her relationship with my father. They are together again; they are a married couple again. To say God works in mysterious ways is an understatement. His purpose and plan are perfect, even when the process does not make sense. Just because my route changed, it doesn't mean my destination has. I won this race.

Mom and Dad, I thank God for both of you in my life! Things were never perfect, but by God's grace and mercy, we're now stronger than ever! May His grace and love continue to show us that family is truly a gift, and one to always be grateful for. I love you!

Edward

Authors notes:

"The closest thing to God's love is a Mother's love."
Laidley Baptist Church

For many children who grow up in this world, the Mother was the most loving parent! The parent that would hug and kiss you and tell you it's going to be alright. The one person who you knew deep down in your heart that no matter what you did, she would forgive you and still love you!

We all need someone like that in our lives, but not all the time do we have that kind of Mother. Sometimes it's the Father who is the most loving parent and the Mother who is the disciplinarian.

Sometimes no parent is around and we only hope that someone else could fill that role for us. Hopefully an Uncle, Aunt, Grandparent, or Mentor, we'd even settle for a stranger. One person who would finds it in their heart, to love us unconditionally like a loving Mother could.

However, it doesn't always happen that way for all of us! Life happens, and we are left to deal with the consequences, choices, and decisions of our parents! Our cards are now on the table, and we can't change that hand that was dealt to us!

Many will complain and blame for the bad hand. Some will give up and say it's just not fair. But a very few will look at their hand and say it's possible, I can still win!

No matter where we are in life or how bad we think our situation is, we still have a choice to make! Instead of looking for someone or something to solve our problems, to give us the love that we never had or reshuffle our deck to give us a better hand, let's take a closer look at the only love that truly matters, the only true forgiveness, the only true success and happiness! One word; "GOD." Just because we don't see Him doesn't mean He isn't with us, and within us!

Like the poem "Footprints," the time that we think we are the loneliest, forgotten, hated, and not loved, that is the time when God is carrying us, loving us, protecting us, and leading us to a victory! All we need to do is let go and allow God to do what He does best; "LOVE."

When we think of our Mother, for the majority of people, we think love, caring, and kind! So many of us in this world never had both parents in the house, and our Mother's had to play the role of Mom and Dad.

This is in some way why I believe Mother's day is so special for a lot of us, because we get to remember and celebrate the woman we love and respect so much in life. No matter what the struggles or challenges, she rose to the challenge and overcame the odds. Our Mothers are in so many ways superhuman, our real-life superhero!

So, what about our Fathers? Without them, we wouldn't be who we are either! Men have always, and will always, play an important role in a child's life, as equal, and in some ways greater than the mother.

"The most important thing a father can do for his children is to love their mother." ~ Theodore Hesburgh

The Father is the example that most children see as strength, authority, leadership, and discipline. Most Fathers, as a default in most cases, has always been the head of a family, the provider, and protector! It's a massive task that has even greater responsibilities!

"A good father is one of the most unsung, unpraised, unnoticed, and yet one of the most valuable assets in our society."
-Billy Graham

CHAPTER 22

Finding Courage

As a child, I was the one who got into any and everything. I was very rambunctious, curious, and always had something to say. In fact, my family gave me two nicknames: Bad Eye and Tornado. I was always in a fight with someone at school or at home with my sister or brother. My personality was so strong that it bothered many adults that I was in contact with. In first grade, I was sent to the office for allegedly stealing a piece of chocolate candy that a boy gave to me. He gave me the candy and then got upset because I ate it. After I began eating it, he tried to take it, and I pushed him down to the ground. Needless to say, I was sent to the office. I was attending a Catholic school at the time, and my principal was a nun. I remember her praying over my head like I was a demonic child or something! I was then sent home for the rest of the day.

It wasn't until I reached the third grade that I started liking school. My first and only African American male teacher called me to his desk and spoke positive words to me. It was during the time of Jessie Jackson—peace and love for all. My teacher looked at me and said these words, "You are smart and beautiful, but most importantly, you can do *anything* you set your mind to because "YOU ARE SOMEBODY!" From that day on, I began making better grades and feeling good about myself. You see, I'm sure my family thought these things, but I was never told. My self-esteem grew from that day on, but it wasn't until I reached high school when I really saw the difference that statement made.

Hi, I'm April, and I'm writing my Chapter so that everyone reading this will understand my trials, my defeats, my tribulations, but most importantly, "My Journey!"

I wear the shoes of many of my family members: My mother, my father, my uncle, my aunts and my teacher. However, my chapter focuses on the power and strength of my mother. You see, I won the race in the shoes of my mother because my mother pushed me. She pushed me in ways that I can't completely describe. My mother is ambitious and outspoken, but most importantly, she has a very giving heart. Because she has such a giving heart, she will put many before herself, making her a selfless person.

Growing up like many teenagers, I didn't always make the right decisions. I was very rebellious toward my mother and father, but mainly my mother. There were many times I wanted to run away from home, but I didn't because I didn't have any place to run to. I'm sure at times my mother wanted the same thing for me as well. I recall the two of us getting into a heated quarrel. I was blamed for doing something I never did. My mother accused me of acting "fast" and not making the right decisions. She thought I had had sex with my boyfriend. I kept telling her that I didn't, but I know she didn't believe me. My mother then called me out of my name and slapped me. Not thinking and just reacting, I slapped her back as I was crying. My father then stepped into the room to see what was going on. I then burst into tears yelling out, "when I get the chance, I'm leaving and never coming back home, I hate it here!"

To this day, I think about those harsh words that came out of my mouth. How hurtful and bitter I was. God only knows how I wish I could take them back. Seeing my mom and dad grow older and me not coming back home to visit like I should still haunts my soul!

That year, I left for college. I was so excited just getting away from home and being out on my own. College was my escape to my world of tranquility! At this point, my escape from home. College was pure freedom for me. A freedom I'd always wanted but had never been given. Unfortunately, that freedom prevented me from completing four years of my academic scholarship. In fact, I only completed one year of college. I'm sure my parents were disappointed, and perhaps embarrassed. They never told me, but my heart knew it, and I felt it! The letdown I gave them has always stuck with me. Being on a four-year academic scholarship and completing only one year before dropping out was enough to embarrass any parent. Why? All because of me wanting freedom and chasing love. Yes, I said it, "chasing love." I met a guy from the Army while in college who showed me attention. Being only seventeen at the time, his attention confused me with love and being in love so much that by the time I turned eighteen, we were getting married. He sent for me to come and visit his family. I thought it was great meeting a guy's parents! Unfortunately, realization kicked in soon that the man I thought I loved didn't love me! Needless to say, he cheated, and this was only the beginning of failed relationships and feelings of me being a failure to my parents. After all, every child wants to make their parents proud. I had failed! Dropping out of college and following a broken love was not the direction or path any parent would want their child to take.

I came back home with the feeling of hurt, abandonment, embarrassment, and the weight of a heavy heart of disappointing my parents, especially my mother. My mom always gives everybody advice, even when we didn't think we needed it! The advice my mother would tell me was, "Get your education and have your own." Her advice was my subconscious. It stayed in my head. My mother is a perfect example of a strong black woman who has always worked hard, fought for her dreams, and got her education. Because of her life struggles and the pain my mother endured trying to pursue her dreams and happiness, this gave me the strength, ability, and motivation to continue my education.

After thinking long and hard. I decided I had to get on the right path with my life. I needed to make my parents proud of me. Most importantly, I had to make my momma proud of me again! I had to change my life for the better. Being at home made me feel uncomfortable and unhappy. So, I decided to join the Navy! I felt that joining the military would get me back on the right path. After all, my sister had joined the Navy, and she was doing well.

I left home, and the things that were permeating through my head had me crying on the plane. I've always tried to hold back my tears and be strong. After all, nobody wants to see tears. I believed tears were a sign of weakness. So, I wiped my tears away and looked forward to my future.

I made it to Orlando, Florida. This was where I was stationed for Boot Camp. The first week of Boot camp, I met a young man with a last name I'd never forget! I began to taste freedom again as I met new friends, both male and female. The air was different, and the people were different. I was loving it!

A year later, I was in love again. As the group Shalamar sang, "Second Time Around," I knew this was the one. He was dark and handsome. I met his family and friends. The next thing I knew, I was getting married. I was so excited!

That young man with the last name I'd never forget became my husband at the age of twenty. I came back home and got married. However, the man I married did not ask my father for his approval. I didn't care at the time about my dad's approval. After all, I found somebody who loved me enough to ask me to marry him. At that time, that was all that mattered, "being loved."

My husband and I moved to Florida because that's where he was stationed. A few months after we were married, my husband went out to sea. When he left for his six-month deployment, he didn't leave me a power of attorney. The car broke down, and I dropped it off to get it fixed. However, when I came to pick it up, they would not give me the car because I had no proof that the car was mine. I had to reach out to an ombudsman to get in touch with my husband. When my husband returned from his deployment, he told me he was written up for not handling his responsibilities. That's when the abuse began. He was drinking a bottle of Tequila. My husband pushed me, and I fell onto the floor. Then, with his uniform boots on, he took his foot and started kicking me. He jammed his foot into my back and side. The neighbor downstairs of our apartment called the police. The police came and took him to jail. The abuse started early in our marriage, but like a lot of abused women, I chose to stay.

A few months later, I was pregnant with our first child. Unfortunately, it was a fetal demise. I was five months pregnant when my baby's heart stopped beating. A year later, I was pregnant again. This time we were successful. We had our first child, It was a girl! We named her after my husband. The girl version of his name.

I truly loved being a wife and mother. It's a feeling that I never wanted to lose. The feeling of security, home, and forever love. Two years later, we had our second child, this time it was a boy. We finally had a complete family. I decided that two would be enough because both pregnancies were high risk.

The years passed by fast. My husband did a lot of sea time so that he would make rank and prosper within his career. Sometimes I would only see my husband five months out of a year. Unfortunately, those five months were not consistent. It began to take a major toll on our marriage. That's when it got worse—the abuse! This time it was verbal. My kids even heard it, especially my son, whom I believe was the most impacted.

It was a total of twenty years we spent together, and no one knew of the abuse. My mother's voice began to speak to me. That's when I knew it was time to separate. It was time for a divorce.

My mother always told me to have my own and get an education. I made a promise to my mother that I would go back to school after I married my husband. It took me thirteen years to get that education, but I got it! Thanks to my mother, I surpassed the bachelor's degree; I pressed on to complete my master's, and I am currently working on the completion of my doctorate.

I can now say that I've won the race. The race in my mother's shoes. The woman who, no matter what, continued to believe in me and remind me to always have my own and get an education. She inspired me, and I will always be thankful for her.

Mom, if you ever get the chance to read this chapter, read about my life and my journey, I would like to say these words from my heart, "Thank You! Thank You! And Thank You!"

I say thank you three times; "Thank You for pushing me. Thank you for constantly reminding me to always have my own and get my education. But most importantly, Thank You Mom for always believing in me and having my back when no one else did.

My favorite Bible verse, "I can do all things through Christ which strengthens me", Philippians: 4:13.

Mom, I Love You Always!

Your Daughter,

April

Author's notes,

> *"The secret of happiness is freedom. The secret of freedom is*
> *courage."*
> *~ Carrie Jones*

Many times, we seek freedom, but the freedom that we think we really want isn't always the freedom that we get.

True freedom isn't an easy road, it's a mountain, it's filled with bumps, bruises, tears, fears, blood, sweat, and sacrifices, to name a few.

> *"Freedom means the opportunity to be what*
> *we never thought we would be."*
> *~ Daniel J. Boorstin*

Freedom also means to accept, who we are, despite what others may think. It allows us to create in our mind a vision for a brighter future. Freedom is accepting what happened in the past can't be changed. It's knowing that no matter what life throws at us next, we can and will confront it head on. It's knowing the only entity to fear is God, and if He stand with us, who can stand against us?

When we're young, the decisions that we make sometimes reflect the emotions that we are feeling. These feelings sometimes lead us to make decisions that we have to live with for the rest of our lives.

"What we think or what we know or what we believe is in the end of little consequence. The only thing of consequence is what we do."
~John Ruskin

CHAPTER 23

Fearing Surrender

I have spent my whole life living how others expected me to live. I was making excuses for people who were supposed to be there to protect me, love me, accept me, with no effort. I ran from those who did this effortlessly. I have always seen the true side of others, but I listened to their stories and gave them reason to be callous, sneaky, I built their emotions into my own. I saw my mother in physical altercations, I was molested, date raped, and pregnant at fourteen. I saw my mother try and commit suicide by slashing her wrists, as if me and my brother were not upstairs in our beds. If I could watch my mother go through and do all the things that I saw and make her the best mother in the world, then why not do that for others?

She was and is a loving and giving woman, I swear, and we know our parents do the best that they can, because we as parents strive to do the same. It just does not work out that way sometimes. But, if I was able to see a better part of others, if they just had one, just one person who could or would love them as they were, then maybe they would change for themselves, not for me. I have had to change colors so many times, I forgot my own shade.

I am thirty-eight, divorced, and I have three girls. I had a mild stressed/drug induced stroke at the age of twenty-eight due to alcohol, stress of a divorce, and drugs. I didn't even know I had this stroke until three days later when I passed out at work. This was my wake-up call.

My name is Navida M, I started off in life, as all little girls do, walking in my mother's shoes. Once we moved from Ohio to Virginia, things changed. Always though, she was so giving. A friend of mine did not have money for a homecoming dress, she bought one. She provided all that she could for my brother and I. When I turned thirteen, my perspective changed a little bit. Her problems were pouring into mine, and I was to blame for certain things (so much goes into this). So, I started walking in others' shoes. I did not know where or who I was to be, it was not at home, it wasn't over there. I gravitated to wherever I needed to that was giving me comfort.

For a little while it was friends' houses, their family dynamic was all that I needed and wanted. At thirty-eight now, I have realized that it is my shoes that I was walking in my whole life, but they were worn down, tired, falling apart. So, I had to get a new pair. I realized that no matter what I do for others, the amount of love, sacrifice, or excuses that I give, they will be who they are regardless. I cannot expect anyone to give me what it is that I am missing if I cannot give it to myself. I walk in my own shoes.

Along the way though, I have had several people who have been in my path, heard my calls when I wasn't speaking. Most of the people I gravitated to had families and belief in God. They opened my eyes to knowing that you are never alone. Instilled in me that for sure, that was not my path.

I have surrendered myself twice completely to God, and when I did, the impact, the feelings that I had, I didn't understand, so I ran. I was/am afraid of it. I know that the moment I surrender myself wholeheartedly to Him, I will no longer be in the control that I believe myself to be. I know that in that moment, my knees will go weak, my heart will begin to race, my tears will fall. I know I am His child; I know that He has been guiding me, but I was too stubborn, too afraid to surrender. Here again, in a place that is all too familiar to me, I look to Him, but I look to the ground instead of with my head held high.

I am smart, funny, independent, understanding, willing, and able. This is how I should see myself. All that I see are my self-inflictions, pulling the reasons out of me that keep me in my own prison. People see my beauty on the outside and fail to see who I am within. I was taught to look down, don't look a man in his eyes, don't raise your voice.

I know that everyone has a story. This is how I have survived the life that I have. Most of the time, my life was guided by others, but I cannot put a blame on them. Simply because I knew they were wrong, but I stayed. I gave them reason! I used to think these things made me weak, because I cry over everything, I keep getting on this train that has no stop. One day, I will see that reflection in the mirror that I look for every morning and every night.

I stopped looking down.

I fell so many times. It wasn't when my mother turned her back on me or when my husband left me for the third time, not when I did the little time in jail, or even immediately after I had my stroke ten years ago. Maybe it was a combination of those things. I got tired of always being sad over the things that did not matter really. The acceptance of others, that fairy tale life that I grew up watching on television. I woke up one day, not feeling like a seventeen-year-old child, and I felt like the thirty-eight-year-old that I am. I looked around at all that I have built on the tears, bruises, empty nights. I looked at my girls who are twenty, sixteen, and twelve, and I thought to myself, where did the time go? I blinked, and I am twenty years into my current life, and I have missed so many beautiful moments in their capacity, because I was looking down.

We all have those life learned lessons that we grow from, that mold us into the people that we see. For me, I have been the same person my whole life, nothing made or broke me. It was the path that I chose for myself. Surviving it is what makes me, me.

Life made me get up from my fall. Not a man, friend, sibling, parent, or child for that matter, could have made me change my frame of thought. It was me, I had to. I saw that reflection and realized that all that ugly that had spilled into me as I went through life was not what I saw in the mirror. I did not have to be envious of the lives that the people I kept around lived.

Behind every closed door is a person's own HELL if they see it to be. I looked at my girls and realized that so much time has gone by, and I cannot waste another minute on the what if this or that. I hear the people who really do have it in my best interest to be at my fullest capacity and know that I got this. When I lay in my bed at night and cry and relive my whole day, the what if's, I secretly call His name, ask Him to forgive me, ask Him my purpose, pray for the strength to get through. Most importantly, I ask Him to protect everyone, my enemies, my loved ones, people I do not even know, and I thank Him.

My race is not over yet, baby! I am eight months away from receiving my bachelor's degree in Health Sciences, I am also eight months away from receiving my certification for Medical Coding and Billing. I am every day away from making myself into all that I have ever wanted to be. My future holds nights with my girls, because all I have ever done is worked and school, so my time is so tight when it comes to being a mother, and the one that I want to be. I do not want to be just the provider; I want to be their mother. I want to build a stronger bond with them.

All of the people who let me into their lives and gave me pieces of their families, I am forever grateful. I know that they always tried to uplift me and to show me what I was not seeing in myself. I do the same for others in the method of 'paying it forward.' Everybody needs or wants something from somebody. I have the examples and hard knock life lessons that I forced onto myself. I make sure to tell my girls to watch me as I go day by day, and I ask them if they want it to be this hard for them. My girls teach me more than I do them, in my belief. I see them at their ages as they are, and I look at how I was then, and it makes me proud, because they are stronger, they have their own mind, their own opinions about things. I strive for them.

There are so many people I could thank in my life. First and foremost, I would thank God, for when I thought that I was alone, He was/is holding me, then I would say to myself: Dear Navida, thank you. I just want to thank you for not fully giving up in life. I want to thank you for every day that you woke up and put your feet on the ground to start off your day for making it, even if you had to fake it. Aryona, Constance, and Korrie, I thank you for choosing me to be your mother. I thank you for the strength that you give me every day to make life a little better than the day before, to be able to get you a little closer to the excellence that is you. I want to thank the certain people in my life who have inspired me, held my shoulder when I did not know, for never giving up on me when I gave up on myself for so long. Loverline Hutchinson, Antionne and Andrea Phillips, Lisa and Bruce Truesdell, Dorothy Mooney, Donald Austin, Ms. Wanda Austin, Professor Absoro Soloman, Professor Dimetrice Jones, and that little girl who lost her innocence at such a young age, thank you for staying strong and by my side.

Author's notes,

"I have known hardship, I have lost myself. But here I stand, still moving forward, growing stronger each day. I will never forget the harsh lessons in my life. They made me stronger."
~lessonslearnedinlife.com

Some people endure things in their lives that the average person would break in pieces if they ever walked in that person's shoes.

We sometimes look at our lives and feel as if we've been given an unfair sentence to suffer! So many things that could go wrong, end up worse, and the time that we thought it was finally getting better, here comes one more problem!

It's hard to be motivated when we think that everything, and everyone is trying to break us. We tend to put up safeguards, and barriers in every part of our lives, especially our heart.

When we find it hard to trust people, it's because we've been disappointed by so many people who have hurt us deeply. When we meet new people, it's difficult to give them a fair chance, because the slightest uncomfortable thing that they do, it becomes a trigger in our mind to run, to close the gates, and get ready for war.

If we live our lives this way all the time, it will keep us isolated, afraid, and stuck on the past. I've learned in life that the only way to not have this problem is to ensure that God is our number one!

Anytime that we put God as our number one option and choice, we can't fail, and most importantly, He'll never fail us! The times that we believe it's all up to us is the time we invite struggle into our lives!

> *"Those who leave everything in God's hands*
> *will eventually see God's hand in everything."*
> *~ Unknown*

We may've accomplished some things on our own and got through some struggles in life! However, imagine how much more we could've done and how much more we can do if we put God first. Imagine how easier the solutions would come to the struggles that we face if we learned to give them to God instead of coming up with our own answers.

We have many races to run in our lives. When we run them with God, the victory isn't for a moment, it's for eternity.

*"Trust the past to God's mercy, the present to God's love,
and the future to His providence."*
~Augustine

CHAPTER 24

MY CHAPTER

It's your turn. This is your opportunity to honor someone who you care about, love, and respect while you still can.

It's your turn to remind them of how much you care about them.

It's your turn to be open, honest, and vulnerable.

It's your turn to say thank you for who they are, what they mean to you, and what they've done for you.

It's your turn to write your chapter and give them a gift like no other—LOVE!

God Bless you on your journey.

Chapter Outline Example

- A situation or story that started the change in how you viewed life or people in it. (*I watched as my father beat my mother, I was arrested for a crime I didn't commit, My father or mother left us, etc,*)

- Who are you: Give your name (*I'm _____, and this is my story, my chapter, etc*)

- Who shoes did you wear: Mother, Father, Aunt, Uncle, Family member, or Mentor! (*I won my race in the shoes of my _____*

- - Give a brief description of you who you are writing about: (*My Mother, etc, is a strong minded person, loving, strict, but fare, etc*) example...........

- How did you fall, what direction were you headed that needed guidance: (*I started hanging around the wrong people, I started to fail in school, I got pregnant, I started to blame my Mother, Father, etc,*)

- Why did you get up from the fall, Why did you start to change your life, and how did this individual or individuals help you? (*I didn't want to go down the same path as my other friends or family, I realized that my Mother or Father, were doing the best that they could for our family, I saw My Mother crying and praying for me to be better, I wanted to do more for my Mother, Father who sacrificed everything for us, etc,*)

- How did you win the Race, Where are you now in you life, and where do you see yourself in the future: (*I graduated high school, I have two beautiful kids that I love more than anything, After I got out of jail I turned to God and have a beautiful family, I have my own business, I have a great job, etc,)*

- What are the things you always remember or advice from your special person that always stuck in your mind, the things that gave you strength, thing that you tell your children or always reference back to in order to help others
  a. My mother would always say, manners will carry you through the world
  b. My Father would always say learn the rules of the game, before you try to change them
  c. My Grandmother would tell me, there are always two sides to a coin, etc.

- Write your thank you letter to your special person, write as if it's the last thing they will ever hear from you: *(Thank you for never giving up on me, God truly blessed me with a Mother or Father like you who never gave up on me, I wouldn't be where I am in life today without your love, I pray that God continues to, etc.*

CHAPTER 24

Story

_____

_____

_____

_____

_____

_____

_____

_____

_____

_____

_____

I am

_____

_____

_____

_____

I won the race in

_____

_____

_____

_____

_____

_____

_____

My fall –

_____

_____

_____

_____

_____

_____

_____

Why did I get up

_____

_____

_____

_____

_____

_____

_____

_____

_____

_____

How I'm winning the race

_____

_____

_____

_____

_____

_____

_____

_____

Things I learned from you

_____

_____

_____

_____

_____

_____

_____

_____

Thank you

_____

_____

_____

_____

_____

_____

_____

_____

_____

_____

_____

_____

_____

_____

_____

_____

_____

_____

_____

_____